Mittens

D1358399

First published in the UK in 2007 by
Collins & Brown
10 Southcombe Street
London
W14 0RA

An imprint of Anova Books Company Ltd

Stitch Style: Mittens

Copyright © Collins & Brown
Text copyright © Collins & Brown

Commissioning Editor: Michelle Lo
Design Manager: Gemma Wilson
Photographer: Mario Guarino
Designer: Clare Barber
Assistant Editor: Katie Hudson
Illustrator: Kang Chen
Senior Production Controller: Morna McPherson

Reproduction by Spectrum Colour Ltd, UK
Printed and bound by SNP Leefung, China

Martingale & Company
20205 144th Ave. NE
Woodinville, WA 98072-8478 USA
www.martingale-pub.com

Printed in China
07 06 05 04 03 02   8 7 6 5 4 3 2 1

Library of Congress Cataloging-in-Publication
Data Is Available

ISBN: 978-1-56477-828-4

MISSION STATEMENT

We are dedicated to providing quality products
and service by working together to inspire
creativity and to enrich the lives we touch.

stitch*style*

Mittens

Twenty
Fashion
Knit and
Crochet
Styles

Martingale®
& COMPANY

Introduction

From trendy teenage girls to thirtysomething professionals, everyone is hand stitching these days. **Stitch Style Mittens** is a collection of contemporary and urban projects that'll keep you constantly inspired and motivated! There's a style here for every season and occasion. Best of all, the projects are portable so you're free to knit anywhere you go.

Stitch Style Mittens is designed for fashion-loving handcrafters and features an array of memorable styles inspired by everything from catwalks to street fashion. All designs are created by talented knitters and trendsetters with a penchant for craft.

Contents

DESIGNED BY JUDY FURLONG

Spot-On Mittens

See spots before your eyes with these jazzy spotty mitts. The yarn carried across the back of the work makes for a double thickness—and warm, toasty hands!

YARN

Jamieson & Smith *2 ply Jumper Weight* (100% wool; 25 g; 115 m) in the following amounts and colors:

MC: 2 balls of color 1A Cream

A: 1 ball of color FC37 Deep Blue

B: 1 ball of color FC6 Pink

C: 1 ball of color FC15 Pale Blue

D: 1 ball of color 72 Deep Pink

NEEDLES

US 3 (3.25 mm) knitting needles
US 2 (2.75 mm) knitting needles
2 stitch markers
Yarn needle

GAUGE
---

28 sts and 36 rows = 4 in. (10 cm) in St st on US 3 (3.25 mm) needles

---
TO FIT	**SKILL LEVEL**
Women's size Medium	Intermediate

FINISHED SIZE: 4 in. (10 cm) wide, 9½ in. (24 cm) long

TIPS

• Yarn amounts given are based on average requirements and are approximate.

• *Instructions are written for the left mitten; figures in square brackets refer to the right mitten. Where only one set of figures is given, this refers to both mittens.*

• Carry contrast yarns not in use loosely at the back.

• When working an M1, there is often a choice of two colors because of the yarn stranded at the back of the work. Choose the cream and pick it up from underneath the other color. This tightens the float very slightly, but should not harm the quality of your knitting.

SPECIAL TECHNIQUE

3-needle BO: Hold two LH knitting needles tog with right sides of work facing each other. With a third needle, knit first st on front and back needles tog. Knit next st on front and back needles tog and bind off as normal by bringing loop of first st over second.

PATTERN

Row 1: K24 [30] in MC, pm, M1 in MC, K2 in MC, M1 in MC, pm, knit to end in MC.

Row 2: P1 in MC, *P2 in MC, P2 in A, P2 in MC; rep from * 3 [2] more times, K2 in MC, K2 in A, K1 in MC, sm, P1 in MC, P2 in A, P1 in MC, sm, P1 in MC, P2 in A, P2 in MC, **P2 in MC, P2 in A, P2 in MC; rep from ** 2 [3] more times, P1 in MC.

Row 3: K1 in MC, *K1 in MC, K4 in A, K1 in MC; rep from * 2 [3] more times, K1 in MC, K4 in A, sm, M1 in MC, K4 in A, M1 in MC, sm, K4 in A, K1 in MC, **K1 in MC, K4 in A, K1 in MC; rep from ** 3 [2] more times, K1 in MC.

Row 4: P1 in MC, *P1 in MC, P4 in A, P1 in MC; rep from * 3 [2] more times, P1 in MC, P4 in A, sm, P1 in MC, P4 in A, P1 in MC, sm, P4 in A, P1 in MC, **P1 in MC, P4 in A, P1 in MC; rep from ** 2 [3] more times, P1 in MC.

LEFT [RIGHT] MITTEN

Using US 2 (2.75 mm) and MC, CO 57 sts.
Work in K1, P1 ribbing for 2¼ in. (6 cm), dec 1 st at end of last row. (56 sts)
Change to size 3 (3.25 mm) needles and St st.

THUMB GUSSET

Starting at row 1, work from chart for thumb gusset as follows:

Row 1 (RS): Work in patt 24 [30] sts, pm, M1, K2, M1, pm, work in patt to end.

Row 2: Work in patt 30 [24] sts, sm, work in patt 4 sts, sm, work in patt to end.

Row 3: Work in patt 24 [30] sts, sm, M1, work in patt 4 sts, M1, sm, work in patt to end.

Row 4: Work in patt 30 [24] sts, sm, work in patt 6 sts, sm, work in patt to end.
Row 5: Work in patt 24 [30] sts, sm, M1, work in patt 6 sts, M1, sm, work in patt to end.
Row 6: Work in patt 30 [24] sts, sm, work in patt 8 sts, sm, work in patt to end.
Row 7: Work in patt 24 [30] sts, sm, M1, work in patt to next marker, M1, sm, work in patt to end.
Row 8: Work in patt 30 [24] sts, sm, work in patt to next marker, sm, work in patt to end.
Rep last 2 rows another 6 times until row 20 of chart has been worked and there are 22 sts between the 2 markers.

THUMB

Row 1: K46 [52] sts in MC, turn, CO 2 sts in MC.
Starting at row 2 (WS), work from chart for thumb as follows:
Row 2: Work in patt 24 sts (including 2 newly CO sts), turn, CO 2 sts in D.
Rows 3–19: Starting with knit row, work 17 rows on these 26 sts until row 19 is completed.
Shape top:
Row 20 (WS): *P2tog in MC, P1 in MC, P2tog in D, P1 in MC; rep from * 3 more times, P2tog in MC. (17 sts)
Break off all contrast colors and cont in MC only.
Row 21: K1, *K2tog; rep from * to end of row. (9 sts)
Break off yarn, thread through rem sts, draw up, and fasten off.
Sew seam.

MAIN SECTION (LEFT AND RIGHT MITTENS ALIKE)

Row 1: With RS facing, rejoin yarn (MC), pick up and knit 2 sts at base of thumb and knit to end of row. (56 sts)
Rows 2 to 20: Starting with row 2 (WS), work 19 rows of chart until row 20 has been completed.
Shape top:
Rows 21–34: Follow chart for mitten top from rows 1–14.
Row 35: K1 in MC, K2tog tbl in MC, work in patt 23 sts, K2tog in C, K2tog tbl in C, work in patt 23 sts, K2tog in MC, K1 in MC.
Row 36: Work row 16 of chart, all in MC.
Row 37: K1 in MC, K2tog tbl in MC, work in patt 21 sts, K2tog in D, K2tog tbl in D, work in patt 21 sts, K2tog in MC, K1 in MC.
Row 38: Work row 18 of chart.
Row 39: K1 in MC, K2tog tbl in MC, work in patt 19 sts, K2tog in D, K2tog tbl in D, work in patt 19 sts, K2tog in MC, K1 in MC.
Row 40: Work row 20 of chart.
Row 41: With MC, K1, K2tog tbl, K17, K2tog, K2tog tbl, K17, K2tog, K1.
Row 42: Work row 2 of chart.
Row 43: K1 in MC, K2tog tbl in MC, work in patt 15 sts, K2tog in A, K2tog tbl in A, work in patt 15 sts, K2tog in MC, K1 in MC.
Row 44: Work in patt 16 sts, P2tog tbl in A, P2tog in A, sl this st back to LH needle.
Graft 2 sets of sts tog, changing color according to sts being grafted.

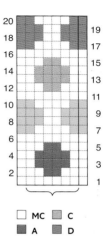

Alternatively, turn mitten inside out and use 3-needle BO.

FINISHING

Darn in loose ends. Pin out according to measurement. Steam or press very lightly using a pressing cloth and avoiding ribbing. Sew side seam.

ON THE SPOT
Why not use a darker color for the main color (MC) of the mitten and add white or cream spots to complement?

DESIGNED BY JENNIFER L. APPLEBY

Slip-Stitch Wrist Warmers

To make these fingerless mitts larger around, try working on a needle the next size up.

YARN

MC: 1 ball of Debbie Bliss *Alpaca Silk Aran* (80% alpaca, 20% silk; 50 g; 65 m), color 12 Purple

CC: 1 ball of Debbie Bliss *Alpaca Silk Aran,* color 20 Pink

NEEDLES

Set of 4 US 8 (5.00 mm) double-pointed needles

GAUGE

18 sts and 23 rows = 4 in. (10 cm) in St st on US 8 (5.00 mm) needles

---

TO FIT	SKILL LEVEL
Women's size Medium	Intermediate

FINISHED SIZE: 7 in. (17.5 cm) wide, 8¼ in. (20.5 cm) long

DOTTED BOX SLIP-STITCH PATTERN

(Worked over 10 rnds)

Work all sl sts purlwise with yarn in back.

Rnd 1: With CC, *sl 1, K5, sl 1, K1; rep from * to end.

Rnd 2: With CC, *sl 1, P5, sl 1, P1; rep from * to end.

Rnd 3: With MC, K1, *sl 1, K3; rep from * to last 3 sts, sl 1, K2.

Rnd 4: Rep rnd 3.

Rnd 5: With CC, K2, *sl 1, K1, sl 1, K5; rep from * to last 6 sts, sl 1, K1, sl 1, K3.

Rnd 6: With CC, P2, *sl 1, P1, sl 1, P5; rep from * to last 6 sts, sl 1, P1, sl 1, P3.

Rnds 7–8: Rep rnds 3–4.

Rnds 9–10: Rep rnds 1–2.

HAMMERHEAD STRIPE SLIP-STITCH PATTERN

(Worked over 10 rnds)

Work all sl sts purlwise with yarn in back.

Rnd 1: With CC, K1, *sl 1, K3; rep from * to last 3 sts, sl 1, K2.

Rnd 2: With CC, P1, *sl 1, P3; rep from * to last 3 sts, sl 1, P2.

Rnd 3: With MC, *K3, sl 1; rep from * to end.

Rnd 4: Rep rnd 3.

Rnd 5: With CC, knit.

Rnd 6: With CC, purl.

Rnds 7–8: Rep rnds 3–4.

Rnds 9–10: Rep rnds 1–2.

RIGHT MITT

Using CC, CO 32 sts. Divide onto 3 dpn: 12, 8, 12 sts.

Rnds 1–5: Work in K2, P2 ribbing.

Rnds 6–8: With MC, knit.

Rnds 9–18: Work dotted box slip-stitch patt.

Rnds 19–21: Rep rnds 6–8.

Rnds 22–31: Work hammerhead stripe slip-stitch patt.

Rnds 32–34: Rep rnds 6–8.

Rnds 35–44: Work dotted box slip-stitch patt.

Rnd 45: With MC, knit.

THUMB OPENING

Rnd 46: With MC, K15. With a 12 in. (30 cm) length of contrasting waste yarn, knit next 5 sts; replace these 5 sts back onto LH needle; with MC, knit across these same 5 sts, knit to end of rnd.

Rnd 47: With MC, knit.

Rnds 48–57: Work hammerhead stripe slip-stitch patt.

Rnds 58–60: Rep rnds 6–8.

Rnd 61: With CC, knit.

Rnds 62–65: With CC, work in K2, P2 ribbing.

Rnd 66: BO loosely in patt.

THUMB

Carefully remove waste yarn at thumb opening; place the 5 sts at the top of the opening on 1 dpn, and the 5 sts at the bottom of the opening on another dpn. Pick up an extra st on each side of thumb opening to make a total of 12 sts. Divide sts evenly onto 3 dpns. With MC, knit 2 rnds. Break MC.

With CC, knit 1 rnd, then work 4 rnds in K2, P2 ribbing.

BO loosely in patt.

LEFT MITT

Work as for right mitt through rnd 45.

THUMB OPENING

Rnd 46: With MC, K10. With a 12-in. (30-cm) length of contrasting waste yarn, knit the next 5 sts; replace these 5 sts back onto LH needle; with MC, knit across these same 5 sts, knit to end of rnd.

Work remainder of left mitt as for right mitt.

FINISHING

Weave in all ends, making sure to close up any holes around base of thumbs.

Textured Gloves

These warm and cozy gloves add a touch of comfort to any outfit.

YARN

4 balls of Debbie Bliss *Alpaca Silk DK* (80% alpaca, 20% silk; 50 g; 105 m), color 15 Yellow

NEEDLES

Set of 5 US 0 (2.00 mm) double-pointed needles

EXTRAS

Cable needle
Stitch markers

GAUGE

14 sts and 16 rows = 2 in (5 cm) in St st on US 0 (2.00 mm) needles

SKILL LEVEL

Intermediate/Advanced

TO FIT

Women's size Medium

FINISHED SIZE

8¾ in. (22 cm) arm length, 6½ in. (15.5 cm) wrist circumference

SPECIAL ABBREVIATIONS

MB (Make Bobble): (K1, YO, K1, YO, K1) into 1 st, turn, P5, turn K5, turn, P2tog, K1, P2tog tbl, turn, K3tog.

SCHIAPARELLI STITCH

(Worked in rnds over an even number of sts)

Crossed st: Knit the second st on LH needle through front loop; then knit first st on LH needle tbl and sl both sts from needle tog.

Rnd 1: *Work crossed st over next 2 sts; rep from * to end.

Rnds 2 and 4: Knit.

Rnd 3: K1, *work crossed st over next 2 sts; rep from *, end K1.

Rep rnds 1–4.

ARM (MAKE 2)

Using long-tail CO method, CO 64 sts onto 1 needle. Divide sts evenly onto 4 needles (16 sts per needle). Join for working in the rnd, being careful not to twist sts, and pm after first st to denote beg of rnd. Knit 1 rnd.

Rnd 1: *P1, K1, P1, MB; rep from * to end.

Rnds 2 and 3: *P1, K1; rep from * to end.

Rnds 4 and 5: Knit.

Rnd 6 (cable rnd): Place 2 sts on cn and hold at back, K2, K2 from cn, *work crossed st over next 2 sts; rep from * to end.

Rnd 7: Knit.

Rnd 8: K5, *work crossed st over next 2 sts; rep from * to last st, K1.

Rnd 9: Knit.

Rnd 10 (cable rnd): As rnd 6.

Rnd 11: As rnd 7.

Rnd 12: As rnd 8.

Rnd 13: Knit to last st, sl last st to RH needle.

Rnd 14 (cable and dec rnd): Place 2 sts on cn and hold at back, transfer slipped st from RH needle to LH needle; K2tog, K1, K1 from cn, transfer second st kw from cn to RH needle, K1, psso, K1, *work crossed st over next 2 sts; rep from * to last st; K1.

Rnd 15: Knit.

Rnd 16: K4, *work crossed st over next 2 sts; rep from * to end.

Rnd 17: Knit.

Rnd 18 (cable rnd): Place 2 sts on cn and hold at back, K2, K2 from cn, K1, *work crossed st over next 2 sts; rep from * to last st, K1.

Rnd 19: Knit.

Rnd 20: K4, *work crossed st over next 2 sts; rep from * to end.

Rnd 21: Knit to last st, sl last st to RH needle.

Rnd 22 (cable and dec rnd): Place 2 sts on cn and hold at back, transfer slipped st from RH needle to LH needle; K2tog, K1, K1 from cn, sl second st from cn to RH needle, K1, psso, *work crossed st over next 2 sts; rep from * to end of rnd.

Rnds 23–86: Rep rnds 7–22 another 4 times. (44 sts)

Rnds 87–97: Knit.

Rnds 98–103: As rnds 7–12.

Rnd 104: Knit.

Rnd 105 (cable rnd): Place 2 sts on cn and hold at back, K2, K2 from cn, *work crossed st over next 2 sts; rep from * to end.

Rnd 106: Knit.

Rnd 107: K5, *work crossed st over next 2 sts; rep from * to last st, K1.

Rnd 108: Knit.

Rnd 109 (cable rnd): Place 2 sts on cn and hold at back of work, K2, K2 from cn, *work crossed st over next 2 sts; rep from * to end. Work should measure about 10 in. (25.5 cm).

Rnd 110 (inc rnd): K4, (M1, K1), knit to last st; (K1, M1).

RIGHT GLOVE
THUMB SHAPING

Next rnd: K4, *work crossed st over next 2 sts; rep from * 9 more times.

THUMB SECTION (TS)

Place next 6 sts onto separate needle, knit these 6 sts and then knit to end.

Next rnd: Knit.

Cable rnd: Place 2 sts on cn and hold at back of work, K2, K2 from cn, K1, *work crossed st over next 2 sts; rep from * 8 more times, K1; **TS:** K6; knit to end.

Inc rnd: K4, (M1, K1), knit to last st, (K1, M1).

Thumb inc rnd: K5, *work crossed st over next 2 sts; rep from * 9 more times; **TS:** (K1, M1), K4, (M1, K1); knit to end.

Next rnd: Knit.

Cable rnd: Place 2 sts on cn and hold at back, K2, K2 from cn, *work crossed st over next 2 sts; rep from * 9 more times, K1; **TS:** K8; knit to end.

Inc rnd: K4, (M1, K1), knit to last st, (K1, M1).

Next rnd: K4, *work crossed st over next 2 sts; rep from * 10 more times, knit to end.

Thumb inc rnd: K26; **TS:** (K1, M1), K6, (M1, K1); knit to end.

Cable rnd: Place 2 sts on cn and hold at back, K2, K2 from cn, K1, *work crossed st over next 2 sts; rep from * 9 more times, K1; **TS:** K10; knit to end.

Inc rnd: K4, (M1, K1), knit to last st, (K1, M1).

Next rnd: K5, *work crossed st over next 2 sts; rep from * 10 more times, knit to end.

Next rnd: Knit.

Thumb inc and cable rnd: Place 2 sts on cn and hold at back, K2, K2 from cn; *work crossed st over next 2 sts; rep from * 10 more times, K1; **TS:** (K1, M1), K8, (M1, K1); knit to end.

Inc rnd: K4, (M1, K1), knit to last st, (K1, M1). (60 sts)

Next rnd: K4, *work crossed st over next 2 sts; rep from * 11 more times, knit to end.

Next rnd: Knit.

Cable rnd: Place 2 sts on cn and hold at back, K2, K2 from cn; K1, *work crossed st over next 2 sts; rep from * 10 more times, K1, knit to end.

Next rnd: K28.

THUMB

TS: K6, take new needle and knit rem 6 sts of TS, take another new needle and CO 6 sts using loop method; close work and cont in St st until approx ⅜ in. (0.75 cm) less than desired length.

Next rnd: (K2tog, K1) 6 times. (12 sts)

Next rnd: K2tog to end. (6 sts)

PALM OF HAND

Pick up 9 sts CO for thumb and knit to end of rnd. (57 sts)

Next rnd: K4, *work crossed st over next 2 sts; rep from * 11 more times, knit to end.

Next rnd: Knit to last st, sl last st to RH needle.

Cable and dec rnd: Place 2 sts on cn and hold at back, transfer slipped st from RH needle to LH needle, K2tog, K1, K1 from cn, sl second st kw from cn to RH needle, K1, psso, *work crossed st over next 2 sts; rep from * 10 more times, knit to end.

Next rnd: Knit.

Next rnd: K5, *work crossed st over next 2 sts; rep from * 10 more times, knit to end.

Next rnd: Knit to last st, sl last st to RH needle.

Cable and dec rnd: Place 2 sts on cn and hold at back, transfer slipped st from RH needle to LH needle; K2tog, K1, K1 from cn, sl second st kw from cn to RH needle, K1, psso; K1, *work crossed st over next 2 sts; rep from * 9 more times; knit to end.

Next rnd: Knit.

Next rnd: K4, *work crossed st over next 2 sts; rep from * 10 more times; knit to end.

Next rnd: Knit to last st, sl last st to RH needle.

Rep last 8 rnds once more.

Note: The number of repeats of crossed stitches diminishes as the stitches on the needle are decreased (i.e., in third decrease round above, work crossed stitch nine times total; in fourth decrease round above, work it 8 times total). Make sure you have a neat line between the pattern and the stockinette stitch on the inside of hand.

Cable and dec rnd: Place 2 sts on cn and hold at back, transfer slipped st from RH needle to LH needle; K2tog, K1, K1 from cn, sl second st kw from cn to RH needle, K1, psso, *work crossed st over next 2 sts; rep from * 10 more times; knit to end. (47 sts)

Next rnd: Knit.

FINGERS

On finishing last rnd, knit first 2 sts of cable and then split sts in half on 2 needles (2 sts of cable on each needle).

LITTLE FINGER

Knit first 6 sts of rnd; using loop method, CO 3 sts onto new needle; transfer 6 sts to spare needle. Sl 1 st from each needle to needle with newly CO sts. (15 sts, 5 sts on each needle) *Work these sts in rnd until you reach 3

rnds less than desired length.
Next rnd: (K2tog, K1) to end.
Next rnd: Knit.
Next rnd: K2tog to end. BO.*

THIRD FINGER

Pick up 3 sts CO for little finger, K5
along upper side of hand, CO 4 sts, K5
along inner side of hand. (17 sts)
Work as for little finger from * to *.

SECOND FINGER

Pick up 4 sts CO for third finger, K5
along upper side of hand, CO 4 sts, K5
along inner side of hand. (18 sts)
Work as for little finger from * to *.

FIRST FINGER

Pick up 4 sts CO for second finger,
K15 along upper and inner side of hand.
(19 sts)
Work as for little finger from * to *.

LEFT GLOVE
THUMB SHAPING
Next rnd: K20.

THUMB SECTION (TS)

Place next 6 sts on separate needle, knit
these 6 sts, and then *work crossed st
over next 2 sts; rep from * 9 more times.
Next rnd: Knit.
Cable rnd: Place 2 sts on cn and hold
at back, K2, K2 from cn, K23, *work
crossed st over next 2 sts; rep from * 8
more times, K1.
Inc rnd: K4, (M1, K1), knit to last st,
(K1, M1).

Thumb inc rnd: K21; **TS:** (K1, M1),
K4, (M1, K1), *work crossed st over next
2 sts; rep from * 9 more times, K1.
Next rnd: Knit.
Cable rnd: Place 2 sts on cn and hold
at back, K2, K2 from cn, K26, *work
crossed st over next 2 sts; rep from * 9
more times.
Inc rnd: K4, (M1, K1), knit to last st,
(K1, M1).
Next rnd: K30, *work crossed st over
next 2 sts; rep from * 10 more times.
Thumb inc rnd: K22; **TS:** (K1, M1),
K6, (M1, K1); knit to end.
Cable rnd: Place 2 sts on cn and hold
at back, K2, K2 from cn, K29, *work
crossed st over next 2 sts; rep from * 9
more times, K1.
Inc rnd: K4, (M1, K1), knit to last st,
(K1, M1).
Next rnd: K33, *work crossed st over
next 2 sts; rep from * 10 more times,
K1.
Next rnd: Knit.
Thumb inc and cable rnd: Place 2 sts
on cn and hold at back, K2, K2 from cn;
K19; **TS:** (K1, M1), K8, (M1, K1); K1,
*work crossed st over next 2 sts; rep
from * 10 more times.
Inc rnd: K4, (M1, K1), knit to last st,
(K1, M1). (60 sts)
Next rnd: K36, *work crossed st over
next 2 sts; rep from * 11 more times.
Next rnd: Knit.
Cable rnd: Place 2 sts on cn and hold
at back, K2, K2 from cn; K33, *work

crossed st over next 2 sts; rep from * 10
more times, K1.
Next rnd: K24.
TS: K6, take new needle and knit rem 6
sts of thumb section, then take another
needle and CO 6 sts using loop method;
close work and cont in St st until approx
⅜ in. (0.75 cm) less than desired length.
Next rnd: (K2tog, K1) 6 times. (12 sts)
Next rnd: Knit.
Next rnd: K2tog to end. (6 sts)

PALM OF HAND

Pick up 9 sts along line of thumb CO
and then knit to end. (57 sts)
Next rnd: K33, *work crossed st over
next 2 sts; rep from * 11 more times.
Next rnd: Knit to last st, sl last st to RH
needle.
Cable and dec rnd: Place 2 sts on cn
and hold at back, transfer slipped st
from RH needle to LH needle; K2tog,
K1, K1 from cn, sl second st kw from cn
to RH needle, K1, psso; K29,
*work crossed st over next 2
sts; rep from * 10 more
times.

Next rnd: Knit.

Next rnd: K32, *work crossed st over next 2 sts; rep from * 10 more times; K1.

Next rnd: Knit to last st, sl last st to RH needle.

Cable and dec rnd: Place 2 sts on cn and hold at back, transfer slipped st from RH needle to LH needle; K2tog, K1, K1 from cn, sl second st kw from cn to RH needle, K1, psso; K28, *work crossed st over next 2 sts; rep from * 9 more times; K1.

Next rnd: Knit.

Next rnd: K31, *work crossed st over next 2 sts; rep from * 10 more times.

Next rnd: Knit to last st, sl last st to RH needle.

Cable and dec rnd: Place 2 sts on cn and hold at back, transfer slipped st from RH needle to LH needle; K2tog, K1, K1 from cn, sl second st kw from cn to RH needle, K1, psso; K27, *work crossed st over next 2 sts; rep from * 9 more times.

Next rnd: Knit.

Next rnd: K30, *work crossed st over next 2 sts; rep from * 9 more times; K1.

Next rnd: Knit to last st, sl last st to RH needle.

Cable and dec rnd: Place 2 sts on cn and hold at back, transfer slipped st from RH needle to LH needle; K2tog, K1, K1 from cn, sl second st kw from cn to RH needle, K1, psso; K26, *work crossed st over next 2 sts; rep from * 8 more times; K1.

Next rnd: Knit.

Next rnd: K29, *work crossed st over next 2 sts; rep from * 9 more times.

Next rnd: Knit to last st, sl last st to RH needle.

Cable and dec rnd: Place 2 sts on cn and hold at back, transfer slipped st from RH needle to LH needle; K2tog, K1, K1 from cn, sl second st kw from cn to RH needle, K1, psso, K25, *work crossed st over next 2 sts; rep from * 8 more times. (47 sts)

Next rnd: Knit.

FINGERS

On finishing last rnd, knit first 2 sts of cable and then split sts on 2 needles (2 sts of cable on each needle).

LITTLE FINGER

Knit first 6 sts of rnd; using loop method, CO 3 sts onto new needle; transfer 6 sts to spare needle. Sl 1 st from each needle to needle with newly CO sts. (5 sts on each needle, 15 sts) *Work these sts in rnd until you reach 3 rnds less than desired length.

Next rnd: (K2tog, K1) to end.

Next rnd: Knit.

Next rnd: K2tog to end. BO.*

THIRD FINGER

Pick up 3 sts CO for little finger, K5 along upper side of hand, CO 4 sts, K5 along inner side of hand. (17 sts) Work as for little finger from * to *.

SECOND FINGER

Pick up 4 sts CO for little finger, K5 along upper side of hand, CO 4 sts, K5 along inner side of hand. (18 sts) Work as for little finger from * to *.

FIRST FINGER

Pick up 4 sts CO for middle finger, K15 along upper and inner side of hand. (19 sts) Work as for little finger from * to *.

FINISHING

Turn gloves inside out and weave in all ends. Turn the gloves RS out again. Soak overnight in soapy water with a few drops of lavender oil (optional).

VARIATION

For a fingerless version, BO at base of fingers and place a button and a loop between ring and middle fingers to hold glove in place. If you choose this option, work only the first few rounds on the thumb and then BO.

DESIGNED BY CLAIRE GARLAND

Rose-Button Gauntlets

These charming crocheted gauntlets have a pretty lace edging at the cuff and a row of tiny crocheted rose buttons at the wrist.

YARN

MC: 1 ball of Lana Grossa *Royal Tweed* (100% wool; 50 g; 100 m), color 26 Pink

CC1: 1 ball of Lana Grossa *Royal Tweed,* color 21 Tangerine

CC2: 1 ball of RYC *Cashcotton 4 ply* (35% cotton, 25% polyamide, 18% angora, 13% viscose, 9% cashmere; 50 g; 180 m), color 902 Pretty

HOOK

Size I/9 (5.50 mm) crochet hook

EXTRAS

Yarn needle

GAUGE

11 sts and 13 rows = 4 in. (10 cm) in single crochet with I/9 (5.50 mm) hook

TO FIT

Women's size Medium

SKILL LEVEL

Beginner/Intermediate

FINISHED SIZE: 9 in. (14 cm) around cuff, 7½ in. (19 cm) long

GAUNTLET (MAKE 2)

Foundation chain (RS): Using CC1 and I/9 (5.50 mm) hook, beg at cuff end, ch 25, turn.

Row 1 (WS): 1 sc in 2nd ch from hook and in each ch across (24 sc); ch 1, turn.

Row 2: 1 sc in each sc across; ch 1, turn.

Rows 3–5: Rep row 2 another 3 times, ending with sl st in last sc to fasten off C, turn.

Row 6: Join MC to sl st (counts as first st), ch 1, 1 sc in each sc across (24 sc); ch 1, turn.

Row 7: 1 sc in each sc across, ending 1 sc in sl st; ch 1, turn.

Row 8: 1 sc in each sc across; ch 1, turn.

Rep last row 5 more times, join with sl st in first sc (does not count as st) to form ring and cont to work in rnds. (24 sc)

Rnd 1 (RS): Sk sl st, 1 sc in each sc around, sl st in first sc.

Rnds 2–3: Rep rnd 1 twice more.

THUMB

Rnd 4: 2 sc in next sc, 1 sc in each of next 23 sc. (25 sc)

Rnds 5–7: Rep rnd 4, inc 1 sc in first sc of next 3 rnds. (28 sc)

Shape thumb:

Rnd 8: 2 sc in next sc, 1 sc in each of next 3 sc, sk next 20 sc, 1 sc in each of next 4 sc. (9 sc)

Cont to work on thumb only.

Rnd 9: 1 sc in each sc around.

Rep last rnd once more.

Fasten off.

HAND

Join MC to rem 20 sc in st at inside edge of thumb, cont to work in rnds to complete hand.

Rnd 1: 2 sc in next sc, 1 sc in each of next 20 sc. (21 sc)

Rnd 2: 1 sc in each sc around.

Rep last rnd 4 more times. Fasten off.

LACY EDGING

Right gauntlet: With front of glove uppermost (thumb facing out toward right), using I/9 (5.50 mm) hook, join CC2 with sl st to sc beneath thumb at opening on right front edge.

Row 1: Ch 1, 1 sc in each of next 13 sc down to cuff on right edge opening (13 sc); ch 1, turn.

Row 2 (WS): Sk first sc, 1 sc in each sc, ending 1 sc in ch 1; ch 1, turn.

Row 3: Sk first sc, *sk 1 sc, 5 dc in next sc, sk 1 sc, 1 sc in next sc, rep from *, ending with 1 sc in last sc. Fasten off.

Left gauntlet: With front of glove uppermost, (thumb facing out toward left), using I/9 (5.50 mm) hook, join CC2 with sl st to sc beneath thumb at opening on left front edge. Work as for right gauntlet, but on left edge opening.

ROSE BUTTONS

Foundation row: Using MC and I/9 (5.50 mm) hook, ch 4.

10 sc in 4th ch from hook, working over loose end. Fasten off, leaving a tail of yarn for sewing onto the gauntlet.

Make 3 more alike in CC1 and 2 in MC.

FINISHING

Use the buttons to join the opening in the gauntlet. Sew 3 buttons as follows: 1 pink at cuff, then 2 tangerine, evenly spacing them to front of lacy edging. When buttons are in position, turn glove inside out and secure yarn at back. Turn right side out.

Driving Gloves

Classic driving gloves made with an incredibly soft lamb's wool—mohair mix add a touch of luxury to even the shortest trip.

YARN

3 balls of Rowan *Kid Classic* (70% lamb's wool, 26% kid mohair, 4% nylon; 50 g; 140 m), color 852 Victoria

---

NEEDLES

US 8 (6.50 mm) needles

EXTRAS

2 buttons of preferred color and size
Stitch holder

GAUGE

20 sts and 20 rows = 4 in. (10 cm) in patt on US 8 (6.50 mm) needles

---

TO FIT

Women's size Medium

SKILL LEVEL

Intermediate

FINISHED SIZE: 4 in. (10 cm) wide, 6 in. (15 cm) long

Note: Use 2 strands of yarn tog throughout—take one end from center of ball and the other from the outside.

LEFT GLOVE

Using 2 strands of yarn held tog, CO 20 sts.

Row 1: Knit.

Row 2: Purl.

Row 3: K2tog, YO twice, K2tog, YO, K12, YO, sl 1, K1, psso, YO twice, sl 1, K1, psso. (22 sts)

Row 4: P1, purl into first of YO and knit into second YO of previous row, P16, purl into first of YO and knit into second YO of previous row, P1.

Row 5: K2tog, YO twice, K2tog, YO, K14, YO, sl 1, K1, psso, YO twice, sl 1, K1, psso. (24 sts)

Row 6: P1, purl into first YO and knit into second YO of previous row, P18, purl into first YO and knit into second YO of previous row, P1.

Row 7: K2tog, YO twice, K2tog, YO, K16, YO, sl 1, K1, psso, YO twice, sl 1, K1, psso. (26 sts)

Row 8: P1, purl into first YO and knit into second YO of previous row, P20, purl into first YO and knit into second YO of previous row, P1.

Row 9: BO 3 sts, knit to end. (23 sts)

Row 10: BO 3 sts, purl to end. (20 sts)

Rows 3–10 form lace edge patt. Keep lace patt correct throughout.

THUMB

Row 11: K2tog, YO twice, K2tog, YO, K9, turn. (14 sts)

Work on these 14 sts only, sl rem sts onto st holder.

Row 12: K1, P11, K1, P1.

Row 13: K2tog, YO twice, K2tog, YO, knit to end, turn. (15 sts)

Row 14: K1, P12, K1, P1.

Row 15: K2tog, YO twice, K2tog, YO, knit to end, turn. (16 sts)

Row 16: K1, P13, K1, P1.

Row 17: BO 3 sts at beg of row, knit to end. (13 sts)

Break off yarn and rejoin to rest of sts.

Next row: K3, YO, sl 1, K1, psso, YO twice, sl 1, K1, psso. (8 sts)

Next row: P2, K1, P4, K1.

Next row: K4, YO, sl 1, K1, psso, YO twice, sl 1, K1, psso. (9 sts)

Next row: P2, K1, P5, K1.

Next row: K5, YO, sl 1, K1, psso, YO twice, sl 1, K1, psso. (10 sts)

Next row: P2, K1, P6, K1.

Break off yarn.

Rejoin 2 sides tog to close thumbhole; work following row with yarn from RH needle.

Next row: BO 3 sts at beg of row, purl to end.

Rep rows 3–9 once more.

Next row: Knit.

BO pw.

RIGHT GLOVE

Work rows 1–10 as for left glove until you reach thumb.

THUMB

Row 11: K2tog, YO twice, K2tog, YO, K3, turn. (8 sts)

Work on these sts only, sl rem sts onto st holder.

Row 12: K1, P5, K1, P1.

Row 13: K2tog, YO twice, K2tog, YO, knit to end, turn. (9 sts)

Row 14: K1, P6, K1, P1.

Row 15: K2tog, YO twice, K2tog, YO, knit to end, turn. (10 sts)

Row 16: K1, P7, K1, P1.

Row 17: BO 3 sts at beg of row, knit to end. (7 sts)

Break off yarn and rejoin to rest of sts.

Next row: Knit to last 4 sts, YO, sl 1, K1, psso, YO twice, sl 1, K1, psso. (14 sts)

Next row: P2, K1, purl to last st, K1.

Next row: Knit to last 4 sts, YO, sl 1, K1, psso, YO twice, sl 1, K1, psso. (15 sts)

Next row: P2, K1, purl to last st, K1.

Next row: Knit to last 4 sts, YO, sl 1, K1, psso, YO twice, sl 1, K1, psso. (16 sts)

Next row: P2, K1, purl to last st, K1.

Break off yarn.

Rejoin 2 sides tog to close thumbhole; work following row with yarn from RH needle.

Next row: BO 3 sts at beg of row, purl to end.

Rep rows 3–9 once more.

Next row: Knit.

BO pw.

FINISHING

Sew widest part of glove tog at back of hand. Make a buttonhole loop at cast-on edge and sew a button on to correspond with buttonhole. Weave in all ends.

VARIATION

Make a pair of driving gloves in a different color for every season.

DESIGNED BY MELISSA HALVORSEN

Sequined Mittens

Sequins or beads sparkle in these fluffy mohair mittens. Either string them directly onto one strand of yarn and pull up a sequin for each knit stitch, or add them afterward using the duplicate stitch.

YARN

A: 1 ball of Rowan *Kidsilk Haze* (70% mohair, 30% silk; 25 g; 210 m), color 579 Splendour

B: 1 ball of Rowan *Kid Classic* (70% lamb's wool, 26% mohair, 4% nylon; 50 g; 140 m), color 844 Frilly

NEEDLES

US 8 (5.00 mm) 12 in. (30 cm) circular needle
Set of US 8 (5.00 mm) double-pointed needles

EXTRAS

Approx 500 sequins, ¼ in. (6 mm)   Stitch holder   Stitch markers

GAUGE

16 sts and 22 rows = 4 in. (10 cm) square measured over St st using US 8 (5.00mm) needles

TO FIT	SKILL LEVEL
Women's size Medium	Beginner

FINISHED SIZE: 4¼ in. (11 cm) wide, 11½ in. (29 cm) long

DUPLICATE STITCH

Bring the threaded yarn needle through the back just below the stitch you would like to cover. In one motion, pick up a sequin and insert the needle under both loops one row above and pull it through, anchoring the sequin to one side of the stitch. Pick up a second sequin and insert the needle back into the stitch below.

MITTENS (MAKE 2)

GAUNTLET

Using 1 strand each of A and B held tog, CO 30 sts. Pm at join.
Work in K2, P1 ribbing for 4 in. (10 cm) or desired length of gauntlet.
Next rnd: Sm, K2, pm. (2 sts between markers)
Next rnd: Knit.

THUMB GUSSET

Next rnd: Sm, M1, K2, M1, sm, knit to end. (4 sts between markers)
Knit 2 rnds.
Next rnd: Sm, M1, K4, M1, sm, knit to end. (6 sts between markers)
Knit 2 rnds.
Cont in this manner until there are 12 sts between markers.
Next rnd (to make up for 2 sts used for gusset): Knit to marker, M1, sm, knit across 12 sts, place these 12 sts on st holder, remove marker, M1.

PALM

Knit 10 rnds.
Rnd 11: Sm, K15, pm, K15.
If using cuff-size circular needles, switch to dpns at this point.
Rnds 12, 14, 16, 18, 20, 22: *Knit to 2 sts before marker, K2tog tbl, sm, K2tog; rep from * once more.
Rnds 13, 15, 17, 19, 21: Knit.
When only 6 sts are left, thread yarn through twice in a clockwise motion and cinch. Thread yarn through center of cinched sts and pull inside.

THUMB

Pick up 12 thumb sts with dpns, twisting the 2 sts closest to the join with the palm to avoid a gap.
Work in St st for 10 rnds or desired length of thumb.
Rnd 11: K2tog around so that 6 sts rem.

FINISHING

Thread yarn through rem sts twice in a clockwise motion and cinch. Thread yarn through center of cinched sts and pull inside.

DESIGNED BY LYNN SERPE

Eyelet Wrist Warmers

These wrist warmers are worked in the round from the cast-on forearm hem to the binding off at the tip of the mitt, all in one piece. The beginning of the round runs up the inside forearms.

YARN

Mitts: 1 ball of Rowan *4 ply Soft* (100% merino wool; 50 g; 175 m), color 372 Sooty

NEEDLES

Set of 4 US 2 (2.75 mm) double-pointed needles
Set of 4 US 1 (2.25 mm) double-pointed needles

EXTRAS

Stitch markers
Stitch holders

GAUGE

28 sts and 36 rows = 4 in. (10 cm) in St st on US 2 (2.75 mm) needles

TO FIT

Women's size Medium

SKILL LEVEL

Intermediate

FINISHED SIZE: 4 in. (10 cm) wide, 13 in. (33 cm) long for fingerless version; 4 in. (10 cm) wide, 12 in. (30 cm) for full version

SPECIAL ABBREVIATIONS

M1L and M1R: See page 68 for instructions.

RIGHT MITT
ARMS
Using US 2 (2.75 mm) dpns, CO 60 sts.

Rnd 1: Knit, dividing sts evenly onto 3 dpns.

Rnd 2: Join for working in the rnd, being careful not to twist sts, and knit around.

Rnds 3–4: Knit.

Rnd 5: Purl.

Rnd 6: (YO, K2tog) to end of rnd.

Rnd 7: Purl.

Rnds 8–11: Knit.

Rnd 12: Fold CO edge under and make hem by knitting tog the CO rnd and the active rnd as follows: using US 1 (2.25 mm) needles, pick up first CO st with RH needle and place it on LH needle, K2tog; cont for entire rnd, picking up next CO st and knitting it tog with next active st.

Rnds 13–15: Using US 2 (2.75 mm) needles, knit.

Rnd 16: K2tog, knit to end.

Rnds 17–19: Knit.

Rnd 20: Knit to last 2 sts, ssk. (58 sts)

Rnd 21: Purl.

Rnd 22: (YO, K2tog) to end.

Rnd 23: Purl.

Rnd 24: K2tog, knit to end.

Rnds 25–27: Knit.

Rnd 28: Knit to last 2 sts, ssk. (56 sts)

Beg patt:

Rnd 29: K13, (K2tog, YO, K12) 2 times, K2tog, YO, K13.

Rnd 30: K12, (K2tog, YO, K1, YO, ssk, K9) 2 times, K2tog, YO, K1, YO, ssk, K11.

Rnd 31: Knit.

Rnd 32: K2tog, knit to end. (55 sts)

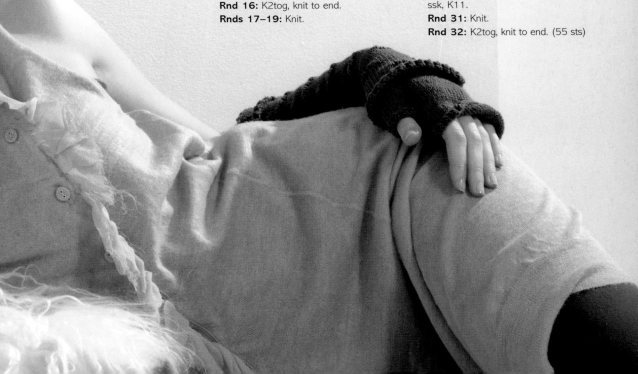

Rnds 33–35: Knit.
Rnd 36: Knit to last 2 sts, ssk. (54 sts)
Rnd 37: K5, (K2tog, YO, K12) 3 times, K2tog, YO, K5.
Rnd 38: K4, (K2tog, YO, K1, YO, ssk, K9) 3 times, K2tog, YO, K1, YO, ssk, K3.
Rnds 39–44: Rep rnds 31–36. (52 sts)
Rnd 45: K11, (K2tog, YO, K12) 2 times, K2tog, YO, K11.
Rnd 46: K10, (K2tog, YO, K1, YO, ssk, K9) 3 times.
Rnds 47–52: Rep rnds 31–36. (50 sts)
Rnd 53: K3, (K2tog, YO, K12) 3 times, K2tog, YO, K3.
Rnd 54: K2, (K2tog, YO, K1, YO, ssk, K9) 3 times, K2tog, YO, K1, YO, ssk, K1.
Rnds 55–60: Rep rnds 31–36. (48 sts)
Rnd 61: K9, (K2tog, YO, K12) 2 times, K2tog, YO, K9.
Rnd 62: K8, (K2tog, YO, K1, YO, ssk, K9) 2 times, K2tog, YO, K1, YO, ssk, K7.
Rnds 63–68: Rep rnds 31–36. (46 sts)
Rnd 69: YO, K14 (K2tog, YO, K12) 2 times, K2, K2tog.
Rnd 70: K1, YO, ssk, K11 (K2tog, YO, K1, YO, ssk, K9) 2 times, K2, K2tog, YO.
Rnds 71–76: Rep rnds 31–36. (44 sts)
Rnd 77: K7, (K2tog, YO, K12) 2 times, K2tog, YO, K7.
Rnd 78: K6, (K2tog, YO, K1, YO, ssk, K9) 2 times, K2tog, YO, K1, YO, ssk, K5.
Rnds 79–84: Rep rnds 31–36. (42 sts)

For shorter arms:
Skip next 16 rnds and go to hand section.

For longer arms:
Rnd 85: YO, K12 (K2tog, YO, K12) 2 times, K2tog.
Rnd 86: K1, YO, ssk, K9 (K2tog, YO, K1, YO, ssk, K9) 2 times, K2tog, YO.
Rnds 87–92: Knit.
Rnd 93: K6, (K2tog, YO, K12) 2 times, K2tog, YO, K6.
Rnd 94: K5, (K2tog, YO, K1, YO, ssk, K9) 2 times, K2tog, YO, K1, YO, ssk, K4.
Rnds 95–100: Knit.

HAND
Rnd 1: (K13, YO, K1, YO) 3 times. (48 sts)
Rnds 2–8: Knit.
Rnd 9: K6, (YO, K1, YO, K15) 2 times, YO, K1, YO, K9. (54 sts)
Rnds 10–16: Knit.
Rnd 17: (K17, YO, K1, YO) 3 times. (60 sts)
Rnds 18–19: Knit.
Beg hem:
Rnds 20–22: Knit.
Rnd 23: Purl.
Rnd 24: (YO, K2tog) to end.
Rnd 25: Purl.
Rnds 26–28: Knit.
Rnd 29: Make hem by knitting tog back of rnd 20 (3 rnds before first purl rnd) and active rnd as follows: using US 1 (2.25 mm) needles, pick up the back of the first st of rnd 20 with RH needle and place it on LH needle, K2tog; cont for entire rnd, picking up back of next st of rnd 20 and knitting it tog with next active st.

FULL MITTS: RIGHT HAND
Rnd 1: Using US 2 (2.75 mm) needles, K40, pm, K10, pm, K10.
Rnd 2 (inc): Knit to first marker, sm, M1R, knit to next marker, M1L, sm, knit to end. (12 sts between markers for thumb)
Rnd 3: Knit.
Rnd 4: Rep rnd 2. (14 sts between markers)
Rnd 5: Knit.
Rnd 6: Rep rnd 2. (16 sts between markers)
Rnd 7: Knit to first marker, remove marker, place 16 thumb sts on holder, remove second marker, CO 2 sts to RH needle, knit to end. (52 sts for mitt hand)
Knit every rnd on mitt until it measures 4½ in. (11.5 cm) from thumbhole or until mitt measures 1⅜ in. (3.5 cm) shorter than desired mitt length.

MITT TIP
Next rnd: K15, pm, K26, pm, K11.
Next rnd (dec): (Knit to 3 sts before marker, ssk, K1, sm, K1, K2tog) 2 times, knit to end.
Next rnd: Knit.
Rep last 2 rnds until 36 sts rem.
Rep only dec rnd until 16 sts rem.
Next rnd: Knit to first marker; cut yarn, leaving a 9 in. (22.5 cm) tail.
Place 8 sts between markers on 1 needle, place other 8 sts on second needle.
BO using kitchener st.

THUMBS (same for both hands)

Place 16 thumb sts on two US 2 (2.75 mm) needles.

With third needle, from base of hand, pick up and knit 4 to 6 sts (depending on how wide you would like the thumbs to be).

Knit all rnds until thumb measures 2 in. (5 cm) or desired length from picked-up sts.

Next rnd: (K2tog) to end of rnd. (10–12 sts)

Next rnd: (K2tog) to end of rnd. (5–6 sts)

Cut yarn, leaving a 4 in. (10 cm) tail. With tapestry needle, weave tail into all rem sts and pull to close. Weave in all tails.

LEFT MITT

Work as for right mitt. If full mitts are desired, work left hand as follows.

FULL MITTS: LEFT HAND

Rnd 1: Using US 2 (2.75 mm) needles, K10, pm, K10, pm, knit to end. Complete left hand as for right hand until you reach mitt tip.

MITT TIP

Next rnd: K11, pm, K26, pm, K15. Complete as for right mitt.

FINGERLESS MITTS

Work right and left hands as for full mitts until hand measures 3 in. (7.5 cm) and thumbs measure ¾ in. (2 cm) or just a bit shorter than your desired lengths, finishing both hands and thumbs as follows:

Next rnd: Purl.

Next rnd: (YO, K2tog) to end.

Next rnd: Purl.

Using US 1 (2.25 mm) needle, BO all sts.

DESIGNED BY KATHERINE HUNT

Striped Mittens

These pretty stripy mittens are the same front and back, so exactly the same instructions are used for both hands.

YARN

A: 2 balls of Debbie Bliss *Donegal Aran Tweed* (100% wool; 50 g; 88 m), color 01 Black

B: 1 ball of Debbie Bliss *Donegal Aran Tweed*, color 04 Natural

---

NEEDLES

US 7 (4.50 mm) knitting needles
US 6 (4.00 mm) knitting needles

EXTRAS

2 large stitch markers
2 small stitch holders (or safety pins)
Darning needle

GAUGE

---

18 sts and 26 rows = 4 in. (10 cm) in St st on US 7 (4.50 mm) needles

---

TO FIT

Women's size Medium

SKILL LEVEL

Intermediate

FINISHED SIZE: 4¼ in. (11 cm) wide, 11 in. (28 cm) long

MITTENS (MAKE 2)

With US 7 (4.50 mm) needles and A, CO 41 sts and work in P1, K1 ribbing for 3 in. (7.5 cm), ending with a WS row. Work 2 rows in St st.

THUMB GUSSET

*Change to B.

Row 1 (RS): K20, pm, M1, K1, M1, pm, K20. (3 sts between markers, 43 sts) Sl markers on each row along with knitting.

Row 2: Purl.
Change to A.

Row 3: Knit.

Row 4: Purl.**

Work in stripe patt from * to **, alternating 2 rows in each color. Do not break yarn between stripes.

Cont inc gusset as on row 1, having 2 more sts inside markers on next row, then every following 4th row to 13 sts between markers. (53 sts)

Work 3 rows even in St st, ending with a WS row in A.

Next row (RS): With B, knit to first marker, sl 13 gusset sts to a holder to be worked later, dropping markers, K1f&b, work to end of row. (41 sts) Cont to work in St st stripes until hand measures 2½ in. (6.5 cm) from top of gusset, ending with a WS row in A.

TOP SHAPING

Break B and cont with A in St st to top of mitten as follows:

Row 1 (RS): K1, skpo, K35, K2tog, K1. (39 sts)

Row 2 and all WS rows: Purl.

Row 3: K1, skpo, K33, K2tog, K1. (37 sts)

Row 5: K1, skpo, K31, K2tog, K1. (35 sts)

Change to size 6 (4.00 mm) needles.

Row 7: K1, skpo, K12, K2tog, K1, skpo, K12, K2tog, K1. (31 sts)

Row 9: K1, skpo, K10, K2tog, K1, skpo, K10, K2tog, K1. (27 sts)

Row 11: K1, skpo, K8, K2tog, K1, skpo, K8, K2tog, K1. (23 sts)

Row 13: K1, skpo, K6, K2tog, K1, skpo, K6, K2tog, K1. (19 sts)

Row 14: BO pw.

THUMB

Sl 13 sts from holder to US 6 (4.00 mm) needle.

Join A and cont to end of thumb:

Next row (RS): K1f&b, knit to last st, K1f&b. (15 sts)

Work in St st for 7 rows.

Shape tip:

Row 1 (RS): (K1, K2tog) across row. (10 sts)

Row 2: Purl.

Row 3: K2tog across row. (5 sts)

Cut yarn, leaving end long enough to sew thumb seam.

Thread end through rem sts. Draw up and fasten securely.

FINISHING

Sew thumb seam. With RS facing, sew side and top seams, taking care to match stripes.

TIP

For neat edges and smooth seams, insert the needle as if to work the next stitch after completing the first stitch in every row. Before completing the stitch, give the working yarn a gentle pull to tighten up the edge, then continue across the row.

DESIGNED BY SUE BRADLEY

Ribbon Arm Warmers

Satin ribbons add a pretty detail to these long wrist-warmer mittens. For some extra sparkle or color, stitch a few beads to the back of the hand.

YARN

2 balls of Rowan Classic Yarns *Soft Tweed* (56% wool, 20% viscose, 14% polyamide, 10% silk; 50 g; 80 m), color 02 Antique

NEEDLES

US 8 (5.00 mm) knitting needles   Tapestry needle
US 10½ (6.5 mm) knitting needles   Stitch holders

EXTRAS

3¼ yds (3 m) of satin ribbon, ⅜–⅝ in. (10–15 mm) wide
Beads (optional)

GAUGE

13 sts and 18 rows = 4 in. (10 cm) in St st on US 10½ (6.5 mm) needles

TO FIT

Women's size Medium

SKILL LEVEL

Beginner

FINISHED SIZE: 4 in. (10 cm) wide, 10 in. (25 cm) long

MITTENS (MAKE 2)

Using US 8 (5.00 mm) needles, CO 28 sts.

Work in K1, P1 ribbing for 10 rows.

Change to size 10½ (6.5 mm) needles and knit 2 rows.

Work 4 rows in St st.

Next row: Knit, wrapping yarn around needle (YO) twice on every st of row.

Next row: Purl, dropping YOs.

With RS facing, work 4 rows in St st.

Make lace holes:

  Next row: *K2, YO, K2tog; rep from * to end.

    Next row: Purl.

     Next row: *K1, YO, K2tog, K1; rep from * to end.

      Next row: Purl.

       Work 2 rows in St st.

        Next row: Knit, wrapping yarn around needle (YO) twice on every st of row.

         Next row: Purl, dropping YO.

THUMB GUSSET (LEFT MITTEN)

  Row 1: K11, K1f&b, K2, K1f&b, K13. (30 sts)

  Row 2: Purl.

  Row 3: K11, K1f&b, K4, K1f&b, K13. (32 sts)

Row 4: Purl.

Row 5: K11, K1f&b, K6, K1f&b, K13. (34 sts)

Row 6: Purl.

For right mitten, work in reverse by beg each RS row with K13 and end with K11.

THUMB (LEFT MITTEN)

Row 1: K21, turn and leave rem 13 sts on st holder.

For right mitten, K22, turn and leave rem 12 sts on st holder.

Row 2: CO 2 sts, P10, turn and leave rem sts on st holder, CO 2 sts. (12 sts)

Row 3: Knit.

Row 4: Purl.

Row 5: Knit.

Row 6: Purl.

Knit 2 rows. BO.

With RS facing, knit across all sts on st holder. (26 sts)

Next row: Purl.

Work 2 rows in St st.

Next row: Knit, wrapping yarn around needle (YO) twice on every st of row.

Next row: Purl, dropping YO.

Work 2 rows in St st.

Knit 2 rows. BO.

FINISHING

Sew in ends and lightly press pieces using a damp cloth. With right sides tog, sew up edges of mitten and thumb seams.

RIBBON DECORATION

Cut 6 lengths of ribbon, 12 in. (30 cm), to thread through the dropped st rows, and 2 lengths of ribbon, 18 in. (45 cm), to thread through the lacy holes. Turn mitten inside out and neatly hand stitch one end of the ribbon to the side seam. Now thread the ribbon into a tapestry needle, or attach a safety pin and use it to thread the ribbon in and out of the lace holes. Stitch the other end of the ribbon carefully to the side seam.

TIPS
- Use a patterned ribbon instead of plain ribbon.
- Lengthen the cuff by working a longer ribbing. (Remember: you will need more yarn!)

DESIGNED BY JUDY FURLONG

Lace Gloves

For plain fingers, ignore the references to bead stitch and work all
fingers in plain stockinette stitch.

YARN

3 balls of Twilleys *Goldfingering* (80% viscose, 20% metallized polyester; 50 g;
200 m), color 31 Ebony

NEEDLES

US 2/3 (3.00 mm) knitting needles

EXTRAS

2 buttons, ¼ in. (1 cm) diameter
2 stitch markers
2 row markers
Yarn needle
Sewing needle and thread

GAUGE

28 sts and 38 rows = 4 in. (10 cm) in St st on US 2/3 (3.00 mm) needles

---

TO FIT

Women's size Medium

SKILL LEVEL

Advanced

FINISHED SIZE: 4 in. (10 cm) wide, 7½ in. (19 cm) long to wrist

BEAD STITCH (BS)

(Multiple of 6 + 1)

This is a traditional Shetland lace patt.

BS row 1: Sm, K2, *YO, sl 1, K2tog, psso, YO, K3; rep from * (number of times stated in patt), YO, sl 1, K2tog, psso, YO, K2, sm.

BS row 2: Sm, K1, K2tog, *YO, K1, YO, K2tog, K1, K2tog; rep from * (number of times stated in patt), YO, K1, YO, K2tog, K1, sm.

BS row 3: Sm, K2tog, YO, *K3, YO, sl 1, K2tog, psso, YO; rep from * (number of times stated in patt), K3, YO, K2tog, sm.

BS row 4: Sm, K1, YO, K2tog, K1, *K2tog, YO, K1, YO, K2tog, K1; rep from * (number of times stated in patt), K2tog, YO, K1, sm.

Pick up and knit 53 sts (approximately 1 st every 2 rows) along nearest (LH) edge of cuff. (54 sts)

Note: When the instructions indicate to work a BS row, remember to work the beg BS sts before the rep, work the rep the number of times indicated, and then work the end BS sts after the rep.

THUMB GUSSET
Inc row (WS): K2, pm, K3, *K1f&b, K5; rep from * 3 more times, pm, K1f&b, K11, K1f&b, K12. (31 sts between markers, 60 sts)

Row 1 (RS): K25, M1, K2, work entire BS row 1 (working rep from * to * 4 times), K2. (61 sts)

Row 2: K2, work entire BS row 2 (working rep from * to * 4 times), purl to last 2 sts, K2.

Row 3: K28, work entire BS row 3 (working rep from * to * 4 times), K2.

Row 4: K2, work entire BS row 4 (working rep from * to * 4 times), purl to last 2 sts, K2.

Row 5: K25, M1, K3, work entire BS row 1 (working rep from * to * 4 times), K2. (62 sts)

Row 6: As row 2.

Row 7: K29, work entire BS row 3 (working rep from * to * 4 times), K2.

Row 8 (mark both ends of this row): K2, remove marker, work entire BS row 4 (working rep from * to * 4 times), remove marker, purl to last 2 sts, K2.

Row 9: K25, M1, K8, M1, K2, pm, work entire BS row 1 (working rep from

SPECIAL INSTRUCTION
When slipping stitches in the following instructions, slip stitches as if to knit.

LEFT GLOVE
CUFF
CO 10 sts. Work 3 rows in garter st.
Lace row 1 (RS): K4, YO, sl 1, K2tog, psso, YO, K3.
Lace row 2: K2, K2tog, YO, K1, YO, K2tog, K3.
Lace row 3: K2, K2tog, YO, K3, YO, K2tog, K1.
Lace row 4: K2, YO, K2tog, K1, K2tog, YO, K3.
Rep last 4 rows 23 more times and row 1 once more, ending with WS facing.
Knit 3 rows, ending with RS facing.
BO 9 sts. (1 st now rem on RH needle)

* to * 2 times), pm, K8. (64 sts)

Row 10: P8, work entire BS row 2 (working rep from * to * 2 times), purl to end of row.

Row 11: Knit to marker, work entire BS row 3 (working rep from * to * 2 times), K8.

Row 12: P8, work entire BS row 4 (working rep from * to * 2 times), purl to end of row.

Row 13: K25, M1, K10, M1, K2, work entire BS row 1 (working rep from * to * 2 times), K8. (66 sts)

Rows 14–16: Rep rows 10–12.

Row 17: K25, M1, K12, M1, K2, work entire BS row 1 (working rep from * to * 2 times), K8. (68 sts)

Rows 18–20: Rep rows 10–12.

Row 21: K25, M1, K14, M1, K2, work entire BS row 1 (working rep from * to * 2 times), K8. (70 sts)

Rows 22–24: Rep rows 10–12, removing both markers on last row.

THUMB

Next row: K41, turn, CO 3 sts.
Next row: P19, turn, CO 3 sts. (22 sts)
Starting with a knit row, work 20 rows in St st on these 22 sts.
Shape top:
Next row: K1, *K2tog, K2; rep from * to last st, K1. (17 sts)
Next row: Purl.
Next row: K1, *K2tog; rep from * to end. (9 sts)
Break off yarn, thread through rem sts, draw up, and fasten off.
Sew seam.

MAIN SECTION

Row 1: With RS facing, rejoin yarn, pick up and knit 5 sts at base of thumb, K10, YO, sl 1, K2tog, psso, YO, knit to end of row. (59 sts)

Row 2: P14, K1, K2tog, YO, K1, YO, K2tog, K1, P10, P2tog, purl to end. (58 sts)

Row 3: K37, K2tog, YO, K3, YO, K2tog, knit to end.

Row 4: P14, K1, YO, K2tog, K1, K2tog, YO, K1, purl to end.

Row 5: K39, YO, sl 1, K2tog, psso, YO, knit to end.

Row 6: P14, K1, K2tog, YO, K1, YO, K2tog, K1, purl to end.

Row 7: As row 3.

Row 8: As row 4.

Rep the last 4 rows.

DIVIDE FOR FOURTH FINGER

Next row: K39, YO, sl 1, K2tog, psso, YO, K9, turn (7 sts rem unworked), CO 2 sts.

Next row: P9, K1, K2tog, YO, K1, YO, K2tog, K1, P30, turn (7 sts rem unworked), CO 2 sts.

Next row: K32, K2tog, YO, K3, YO, K2tog, K9, turn.

Next row: P9, K1, YO, K2tog, K1, K2tog, YO, K1, P32, turn.

FINGERS

FIRST FINGER

Next row: K32, turn, CO 2 sts.
Next row: P18, turn, CO 2 sts. (20 sts)
On these 20 sts only, work 22 rows in St st.

Shape top:
Next row: K1, *K2tog , K2, rep from * to last 3 sts, K2tog, K1. (15 sts)
Next row: Purl.
Next row: K1, *K2tog, rep from * to end. (8 sts)
Break off yarn, thread through rem sts, draw up, and fasten off.
Sew seam.

SECOND FINGER

Row 1: With RS facing, pick up and knit 3 sts from base of first finger, K2, YO, sl 1, K2tog, psso, YO, K2, turn, CO 2 sts.

Row 2: P2, K1, K2tog, YO, K1, YO, K2tog, K1, P1, P2tog, P7, turn, CO 2sts. (20 sts)

Cont on these 20 sts as follows:

Row 3: K11, K2tog, YO, K3, YO, K2tog, K2.

Row 4: P2, K1, YO, K2tog, K1, K2tog, YO, K1, P11.

Row 5: K13, YO, sl 1, K2tog, psso, YO, K4.

Row 6: P2, K1, K2tog, YO, K1, YO, K2tog, K1, P11.

Row 7: As row 3.

Row 8: As row 4.

Rep last 4 rows another 5 times.

Shape top:
Work as for first finger.

THIRD FINGER

Next row: With RS facing, rejoin yarn, pick up and knit 3 sts from base of second finger, K9, turn.

Next row: P10, P2tog, P9, turn. (20 sts)

On these 20 sts only, work 22 rows in St st.

Shape top:

Work as for first finger.

FOURTH FINGER

Next row: With RS facing, rejoin yarn, pick up and knit 3 sts from base of third finger, knit to end of row. (17 sts) Starting with a purl row, work 17 rows in St st on these 17 sts.

Shape top:

Next row: K1, *K2tog, K2, rep from * to end. (13 sts)

Next row: Purl.

Next row: K1, *K2tog, rep from * to end. (7 sts)

Break off yarn, thread through rem sts, draw up, and fasten off.

Sew side seam as far as the garter st edge (at row markers).

RIGHT GLOVE

CUFF

Work as for left glove.

THUMB GUSSET

Inc row (WS): K12, K1f&b, K11, K1f&b, pm, K5, *K1f&b, K5, rep from * 3 more times. (60 sts)

Row 1 (RS): K2, pm, work entire BS row 1 (working rep from * to * 4 times), K2, M1, K25. (61 sts)

Row 2: K2, P26, work entire BS row 2 (working rep from * to * 4 times), K2.

Row 3: K2, work entire BS row 3 (working rep from * to * 4 times), K28.

Row 4: K2, P26, work entire BS row 4

(working rep from * to * 4 times), K2.

Row 5: K2, work entire BS row 1 (working rep from * to * 4 times), K3, M1, K25. (62 sts)

Row 6: K2, P27, work entire BS row 2 (working rep from * to * 4 times), K2.

Row 7: K2, work entire BS row 3 (working rep from * to * 4 times), K29.

Row 8 (mark both ends of this row): K2, P27, work entire BS row 4 (working rep from * to * 4 times) and removing marker, K2.

Row 9: K8, work entire BS row 1 (working rep from * to * 2 times and ignoring references to markers), pm, K2, M1, K8, M1, K25. (64 sts)

Row 10: Purl to first marker, work entire BS row 2 (working rep from * to * 2 times), P8.

Row 11: K8, work entire BS row 3 (working rep from * to * 2 times), knit to end.

Row 12: Purl to first marker, work entire BS row 4 (working rep from * to * 2 times), P8.

Row 13: K8, work entire BS row 1 (working rep from * to * 2 times), K2, M1, K10, M1, knit to end. (66 sts)

Rows 14–16: Rep rows 10–12.

Row 17: K8, work entire BS row 1 (working rep from * to * 2 times), K2, M1, K12, M1, knit to end. (68 sts)

Rows 18–20: Rep rows 10–12.

Row 21: K8, work entire BS row 1 (working rep from * to * 2 times), K2, M1, K14, M1, knit to end. (70 sts)

Rows 22–24: Rep rows 10–12, removing markers on last row.

THUMB

Next row: K16, *YO, sl 1, K2tog, psso, YO, K26, turn, CO 3 sts.

Next row: P19, turn, CO 3 sts. (22 sts) Starting with a knit row, work 20 rows in St st on these 22 sts.

Shape top:

Next row: K1, *K2tog, K2, rep from * to last st, K1 (17 sts).

Next row: Purl.

Next row: K1, *K2tog, rep from * to end of row. (9 sts)

Break off yarn, thread through rem sts, draw up, and fasten off.

Sew side seam.

MAIN SECTION

Row 1: With RS facing, rejoin yarn, pick up and knit 5 sts at base of thumb, knit to end of row. (59 sts)

Row 2: P26, P2tog, P9, K1, K2tog, YO, K1, YO, K2tog, K1, purl to end of row. (58 sts)

Row 3: K14, K2tog, YO, K3, YO, K2tog, knit to end of row.

Row 4: P37, K1, YO, K2tog, K1, K2tog, YO, K1, purl to end of row.

Row 5: K16, YO, sl 1, K2tog, psso, YO, knit to end of row.

Row 6: P37, K1, K2tog, YO, K1, YO, K2tog, K1, purl to end of row.

Row 7: As row 3.

Row 8: As row 4.

Rep last 4 rows.

DIVIDE FOR FOURTH FINGER

Next row: K16, YO, sl 1, K2tog, psso, YO, K32, turn (7 sts rem unworked), CO 2 sts.

Next row: P32, K1, K2tog, YO, K1, YO, K2tog, K1, P7, turn (7 sts rem unworked), CO 2 sts.

Next row: K9, K2tog, YO, K3, YO, K2tog, K32, turn.

Next row: P32, K1, YO, K2tog, K1, K2tog, YO, K1, P9, turn.

FINGERS

FIRST FINGER

Next row: K11, YO, sl 1, K2tog, psso, YO, K18, turn, CO 2 sts.

Next row: P18, turn, CO 2 sts. (20 sts)

On these 20 sts only, work 22 rows in St st.

Shape top:

Work as for left glove first finger.

SECOND FINGER

Row 1: With RS facing, rejoin yarn, pick up and knit 3 sts from base of first finger, K7, turn, CO 2 sts.

Row 2: P9, P2tog, P1, K1, K2tog, YO, K1, YO, K2tog, K1, turn, CO 2 sts. (20 sts)

Cont on these 20 sts as follows:

Row 3: K2, K2tog, YO, K3, YO, K2tog, K11.

Row 4: P11, K1, YO, K2tog, K1, K2tog, YO, K1, P2.

Row 5: K4, YO, sl 1, K2tog, psso, YO, K13.

Row 6: P11, K1, K2tog, YO, K1, YO, K2tog, K1, P2.

Row 7: As row 3.

Row 8: As row 4.

Rep last 4 rows another 5 times.

Shape top:

Work as for left glove first finger.

THIRD FINGER

Work as for left glove third finger.

FOURTH FINGER

Work as for left glove fourth finger.

FINISHING

Weave in loose ends. Pin out according to measurement. Spray lightly with water and allow to dry thoroughly. Sew a loop (single thickness of yarn or chain stitch, see below) at edge of upper glove at wrist (where cuff attaches to glove). Sew a button on edge of palm side of each glove to correspond with the loop—this is easier with sewing thread rather than using the Goldfingering yarn.

CHAIN STITCH LOOP

Secure a length of yarn to the edge of glove. Insert the needle back into the same point and draw up to make a small loop. Insert needle into this loop from underneath and reinsert from top. Gently tighten up the first loop. Rep until chain is desired length to accommodate button. Fasten to glove edge, forming a loop.

TIPS

- Work the last row of shaping for the thumb and fingers tightly or with a finer needle.
- For fingerless gloves, work four rows of the thumb and fingers, then BO.

DESIGNED BY GABRIELLE CARTER

Fair Isle Warmers

Since these fun, fingerless gloves have no thumb gusset, there is no increase at the hand, and the cuff sits loosely on the wrist. The pattern could be knitted in intarsia to make the gloves reversible.

YARN

Debbie Bliss *Cashmerino Chunky* (55% merino, 33% microfiber, 12% cashmere; 50 g; 65 m)

A: 1 ball of color 05 Fuschia
B: 1 ball of color 07 Magenta
C: 1 ball of color 12 Lime
D: 1 ball of color 14 Taupe
E: 2 balls of color 15 Chocolate
F: 1 ball of color 20 Slate
G: 1 ball of Debbie Bliss *Cashmerino Aran* (55% merino, 33% microfiber, 12% cashmere; 50 g; 90 m), color 016 Burnt Orange

NEEDLES

Set of 5 US 7 (4.50 mm) double-pointed needles

GAUGE

18 sts and 23 rows = 4 in. (10 cm) in St st on US 7 (4.50 mm) needles

EXTRAS

Cable needle
Stitch holders
Stitch markers

TO FIT

Women's size Medium

SKILL LEVEL

Intermediate

FINISHED SIZE: 4 in. (10 cm) wide, 10¾ in. (27 cm) long

SPECIAL ABBREVIATIONS

C2B: Sl 1 st onto cn and hold at back, K1, K1 from cn.

TIPS

- As the dimensions are given in inches and centimeters rather than specific rounds, each new sequence begins with round 1.
- Remember to twist the yarn in as the pattern moves; this will make for smaller floats, which is important when trying to fit the gloves correctly.

GLOVES (MAKE 2)
BODY

Using US 7 (4.50 mm) needles, CO 36 sts using the long-tail method. Arrange sts on 4 dpns.

Rnd 1: *K1, P1; rep from * to end of rnd (C2B to secure bridge on this first rnd).

Rep this rnd until the cuff measures approx 2⅜ in. (6 cm)—approx 15 rnds. At beg of next rnd, change to moss st as follows:

Rnd 1: *P1, K1; rep from * to end.
Rnd 2: *K1, P1; rep from * to end.

Rep these 2 rows for 5 rnds, ending on a rnd 1 rep.

Change color and complete 1 full rnd in purl. Work in purl from this point until end of Fair Isle patt (with the exception of 2 rows in the middle). **The patt is knitted in rnds from the inside as rev St st.**

Refer to chart on opposite page for Fair Isle patt and color-change directions. Cont with patt, including 2 rnds of continuous knit (St st) toward the top, until glove body measures 7¾ in. (19.5 cm)—approx 50 rnds.

THUMB GAP

At beg of next rnd, work sts back and forth rather than in rnds. This results in a fork at beg and end of rows.

Cont with Fair Isle patt and moss st on hand throughout these rows, working moss st as established.

Work moss st for 3 rnds until thumb gap measures 1¾ in. (4.5 cm).

To resume rnds, work row up to last st and then sl last st onto a cn and C2B. This should bridge the gap securely and allow you to work in rnds from this point.

UPPER HAND

Cont in moss st for upper hand until it measures 1¼ in. (3 cm) from top of thumb gap, 11 in. (27 cm) total length.

FINGERS

Note that for all fingers you must knit half the sts before you work the sequence, so placement is at opposite end to thumb gap.

LITTLE FINGER

Knit half rnd, K4, place following 28 sts on holder, leaving final 4 sts to work for little finger.

Divide these 8 sts between 3 dpns.

On first rnd, work moss st until reaching gap at hand and C2B (using 2 sts on either side of hand gap).

Cont working little finger in moss st for 2 more rnds, moving into K1, P1 ribbing for final 2 rnds.

BO 8 sts.

So placement of other fingers is slightly higher than little finger, complete 1 rnd before starting on second finger.

Reattach yarn at bridged finger gap to pull gap tog. Work 1 complete rnd.

THIRD FINGER

K4, place next 20 sts on holder, leaving final 4 sts to work for third finger.

Divide these 8 sts between 3 dpns.

On first rnd, work moss st until reaching gap at hand (and between third and little fingers) and C2B.

Cont working third finger in moss st for 3 more rnds, then move into K1, P1 ribbing for final 2 rnds.

BO 8 sts.

SECOND FINGER

Reattach yarn at bridged finger gap, K5, place next 10 sts on holder, leaving final 5 sts to work for second finger.

Divide these 10 sts between 3 dpns.

On first rnd, work moss st until reaching gap at hand (and between third and second fingers) and C2B.

Cont working second finger in moss st for 3 more rnds, then move into K1, P1 ribbing for final 2 rnds.

BO 10 sts.

FIRST FINGER

Reattach yarn at bridged finger gap and make 2 sts by picking up bar at second-finger bridge, leaving 12 sts. Divide these 12 sts between 3 dpns.

On first rnd, work moss st until reaching gap at hand (and between second and first fingers) and C2B.

Cont first finger in moss st for another 4 rnds, then work K1, P1 ribbing for final 2 rnds.

BO 12 sts.

FINISHING

Weave in all ends and reinforce any gaps that may have formed between the fingers.

CHART NOTE

The Fair Isle Warmers are knit in the round and the chart is worked from right to left, but for the sake of legibility, row numbers are shown at both right and left in the chart.

A B C D E F G

 Knit Stitch/ change of color

 Reverse ST st

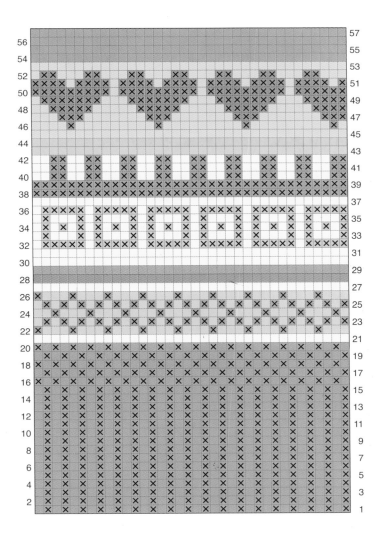

DESIGNED BY SOPHIE BRITTEN

Marshmallow Muff

This gorgeous supersoft hand warmer is knit in a double thickness of sumptuous mohair and sparkle yarn. It can be worn on its own or with a detachable cord that goes around the neck or through a jacket.

YARN

A: 2 balls of Rowan *Romance* (36% acrylic, 27% nylon, 26% mohair, 8% polyester, 3% wool; 50 g; 55 m), color 090 Glitter

B: 2 balls of Rowan *Romance,* color 095 Sparkle

NEEDLES

US 10½ (6.5 mm) knitting needles
US 6 (4.00 mm) double-pointed needles
Tapestry needle

EXTRAS

A piece of stiff paper/cardboard for pom-poms
2 small D rings
2 snap fasteners, 1 ½ in. (38 mm)

GAUGE

12 sts and 16 rows = 4 in. (10 cm) in St st on US 10½ (6.5 mm) needles with 2 strands of yarn held tog

---

TO FIT

Women's size Medium

SKILL LEVEL

Beginner

FINISHED SIZE: 7 in. (18 cm) wide, 12 in. (30 cm) long

MUFF

Using 2 strands of A held tog and US 10½ (6.5 mm) needles, CO 46 sts.

Row 1: Knit.

Row 2: Purl.

Drop A. Use 2 strands of B held tog:

Row 3: Knit.

Row 4: Purl.

Pick up A and cont to work in St st, alternating A and B every other row for 104 rows. BO, leaving a long tail for sewing.

POM-POMS (MAKE 4)

Cut 2 disks of cardboard measuring 1⅝ in. (4 cm) in diameter. Cut a ¾ in. (2 cm) diameter hole in the center of both disks. Cut off approximately 3 yds (270 cm) of A. Place the disks tog; passing the yarn through the center of the hole, wrap the yarn around the outside of the disks, making sure the rings are uniformly covered. Cut the yarn at the edge of the ring, and positioning the scissors between the two pieces of cardboard, cut the yarn all around the ring. Take a piece of yarn 15 in. (40 cm) long and, leaving one short tail and one long, wrap it very tightly around the cut pieces between the two disks and tie a knot. Remove the cardboard disks and fluff out your pom-pom—you may need to trim it to make an even sphere. Trim off the short tail.

STRAP

Using two US 6 (4.00 mm) double-pointed needles and B, CO 3 sts. Slide the sts to the other end of the needle and, carrying the yarn across the back, knit the next row.

Continue to knit and slide in this way until the strap measures 45 in. (114 cm). BO. You may need to give the cord a tug as you pull it into a tube. Do not sew in ends.

FINISHING

With RS of muff facing, sew up the long sides using a mattress stitch; do not fasten off. Fold the muff in half, and you will now have a double-thickness tube. With RS facing, sew up the end as you would an invisible shoulder seam. Weave in all ends. Rearrange the muff so that the seam is centrally placed inside the muff. Attach D rings to either end of the muff. Using the tails, attach the snap fasteners to either end of the strap. Tie two pom-poms onto each side of the strap.

MATTRESS STITCH

With WS facing, lay the fabric flat and fold in the two sides so that they are next to each other, RS facing, with the stitches lined up row for row. Mattress stitch is worked by inserting the needle under the bar between the edge stitch and the one next to it. Using a tapestry needle, insert the needle under the bar of the first stitch on one side. Pull the yarn through and insert the needle under the parallel horizontal bar on the opposite side. Work back and forth until you reach the top. Do not fasten off; you can continue to work the seam at the top of the tube.

INVISIBLE SHOULDER SEAM

Instead of aligning the stitches row by row, work horizontally and align stitch by stitch. Insert the needle behind the first stitch to the left of the seam you have just worked, under the cast-on row on the outer tube from right to left, and bring the needle through to the front of the work. Now insert the needle from right to left behind the corresponding stitch on the inner tube and then bring it through to the front of the work. Alternating from outer to inner, work around the tube.

DESIGNED BY CAROL MELDRUM

Flip-Top Mitts

These are worked in single, half double, and double crochet. Adjust the size by adding more rows before shaping the top.

YARN

2 balls of Rowan ***Tapestry*** (70% wool, 30% soybean fiber; 50 g; 120 m), color 171 Rainbow

HOOK

F/5 (3.75 mm) crochet hook

EXTRAS

Stitch markers
Pins
Tapestry needle

GAUGE

18 sts and 9 rows = 4 in. (10 cm) over dc

TO FIT

Women's size Medium

SKILL LEVEL

Advanced

FINISHED SIZE: 4 in. (10 cm) wide, 8¾ in. (22 cm) long

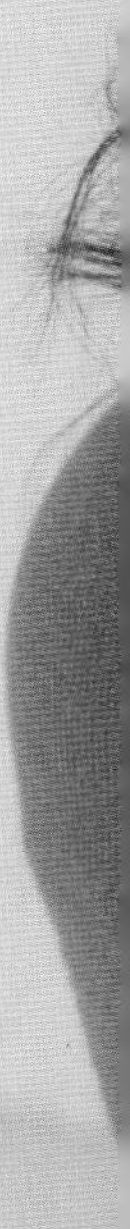

MITTENS (MAKE 2)
BASE
Ch 41.

Row 1: 1 sc into 2nd ch from hook, 1 sc into each ch to end, turn.

Row 2: Ch 1, sk 4 sc, *9 dc into next sc, sk 3 sc, 1 sc into next sc, sk 3 sc; rep from *, ending with 1 sc in last sc, turn.

Row 3: Ch 3, sk first sc, dc4tog over next 4 dc, *ch 3, 1 sc into next dc (center of 9), ch 3, dc9tog over (next 4 dc, 1 sc, 4 dc); rep from *, ending with dc5tog over (last 4 dc and 1 ch), turn.

Row 4: Ch 3, 4 dc in top of dc5tog, *1 sc in sc, sk 3 ch, work 9 dc in top of dc9tog; rep from *, ending with 5 dc in top of dc4tog, turn.

Row 5: Ch 3, sk first dc, *dc9tog over (next 4 dc, 1 sc, 4 dc), ch 3, 1 sc in next dc (center of 9 dc), ch 3; rep from *, ending with 1 sc in top of turning ch, turn.

Row 6: Ch 1, sk first sc, *sk 3 ch, 9 dc in top of dc9tog, sk 3 ch, 1 sc in sc; rep from *, working last sc in top of first 3 ch, turn.

Rows 3–6 form patt. Rep rows 3–6 once more, then rows 3–4 once again. Fasten off.

TOP (MAKE 2)
Ch 35 plus 2 turning ch.

Row 1: Work 1 dc into 3rd ch from hook, work 1 dc into each ch to end, turn. (35 sts)

Row 2: Ch 2, 1 dc into each dc of previous row, turn.

Rep row 2 another 5 times.

TOP SHAPING
Next row: Ch 2, dc2tog, 13 dc, dc2tog, 1 dc, dc2tog, 12 dc, dc2tog, 1 dc, turn. (31 sts)

Next row: Ch 2, dc2tog, 11 dc, dc2tog, 1 dc, dc2tog, 10 dc, dc2tog, 1 dc, turn. (27 sts)

Next row: Ch 2, dc2tog, 9 dc, dc2tog, 1 dc, dc2tog, 8 dc, dc2tog, 1 dc, turn. (23 sts)

Next row: Ch 2, dc2tog, 7 dc, dc2tog, 1 dc, dc2tog, 6 dc, dc2tog, 1 dc, turn. (19 sts)

Fasten off.

THUMB (MAKE 2)
Ch 4, sl st into first ch to form a ring.

Rnd 1: Ch 2, 9 dc into ring, sl st into top of ch at beg of rnd.

Rnds 2–5: Ch 2, 1 dc into each dc of prev rnd, join with sl st into top of ch at beg of rnd.

Rnd 6: Ch 1, 1 sc into next 3 dc, 2 dc into next dc, 1 dc, 2 dc into next dc, 1 sc into next 3 dc, sl st into top of ch 1 at beg of rnd. (11 sts)

Rnd 7: Ch 1, 1 sc into next 3 sts, 2 hdc into next st, 2 dc into next st, 1 dc, 2 dc into next st, 2 hdc into next st, 1 sc into next 3 sts, sl st into top of ch 1 at beg of rnd. (15 sts)

Rnd 8: Ch 1, 1 sc into next 5 sts, 2 hdc into next st, 2 dc into next st, 1 dc, 2 dc into next st, 2 hdc into next st, 1 sc into next 5 sts, sl st into top of ch 1 at beg of rnd. (19 sts)

Rnd 9: Ch 1, 1 sc into next 7 sts, 2 hdc into next st, 2 dc into next st, 1 dc, 2 dc into next st, 2 hdc into next st, 1 sc into next 7 sts, sl st into top of ch 1 at beg of rnd. (23 sts)

Break off yarn.

FINISHING
Weave in all loose ends; block and press fabric. Pm at center point of both mitten top and base. Pin mitten top to inside of mitten base along row 10. Using backstitch, sew into position up to center-point marker.

Fold mitten top in half and stitch top and sides tog. Fold mitten base in half, stitch up to row 4, then stitch tog row 10 and upward—this will leave a gap for your thumb. Pin thumb into position and stitch into place.

Remember when stitching top flap into position that for LH, stitch to RH side of base, and for RH, stitch to LH side of base, to make sure both mittens flip in the same direction.

DESIGNED BY KATHERINE HUNT

Cable Mittens

These warm and cozy mittens have an easy-to-work bobbly cable panel running up the back of the hand.

YARN

2 balls of Debbie Bliss *Donegal Aran Tweed* (100% wool; 50 g; 88 m),
  color 07 Purple

NEEDLES

US 7 (4.50 mm) knitting needles
US 6 (4.00 mm) knitting needles

EXTRAS

Cable needle   2 stitch markers
2 small stitch holders
Darning needle

GAUGE

18 sts and 24 rows = 4 in. (10 cm) in St st on US 7 (4.50 mm) needles

---

TO FIT

Women's size Medium

SKILL LEVEL

Intermediate

FINISHED SIZE: 8 in. (20 cm) around, 11 in. (28 cm) long

DESIGNED BY GRYPHON PERKINS

Accordion Gloves

Keep your hands warm and toasty in these unusual accordion gloves, knitted in the softest silk/wool mix. They are worked in the round, so there are no seams to sew at the end.

YARN

3 balls of Noro *Silk Garden* (45% silk, 45% mohair, 10% lamb's wool; 50 g; 120 m), color 84

NEEDLES

Set of 4 US 6 (4.00 mm) double-pointed needles
Set of 4 US 7 (4.50 mm) double-pointed needles

EXTRAS

Stitch holder

GAUGE

18 sts and 24 rows = 4 in. (10 cm) in St st on US 7 (4.50 mm) needles

TO FIT

Women's size Medium

SKILL LEVEL

Intermediate

FINISHED SIZE: Hand circumference 7½ in. (19 cm)

Bow Belles Mittens

These elegant mittens are knit in one piece and finished with a gorgeous knitted ribbon in a bright contrasting shade.

YARN

A: 1 ball of Rowan *Wool Cotton* (50% merino, 50% cotton; 50 g; 113 m), color 900 Antique

B: 1 ball of Rowan *Kidsilk Haze* (70% super kid mohair, 30% silk; 25 g; 120 m), color 606 Candy Girl

NEEDLES

US 6 (4.00 mm) knitting needles
US 6 (4.00 mm) circular needle
Size C/2 (2.75 mm) crochet hook
Tapestry needle

GAUGE

Mittens: 23 sts and 29 rows = 4 in. (10 cm) in St st on US 6 (4.00 mm) needles
Ribbon: 26 sts and 28 rows = 4 in. (10 cm) in St st on US 6 (4.00 mm) needles

TO FIT

Women's size Small

SKILL LEVEL

Intermediate

FINISHED SIZE: 3½ in. (9 cm) wide, 8 in. (20 cm) long

DESIGNED BY SUE BRADLEY

Clock Wrist Warmers

The frilled cuff on these stylish gloves is optional—it could also be knitted in a contrasting color.

YARN

A: 2 balls of Rowan *Pure Wool DK* (100% wool; 50 g; 122 m), color 004 Black

B: 1 ball of Rowan *Pure Wool DK,* color 012 Snow

C: 1 ball of Twilleys *Goldfingering* (80% viscose, 20% metallized polyester; 25 g; 200 m), color 11

NEEDLES

US 3 (3.25 mm) knitting needles
US 6 (4.00 mm) knitting needles

EXTRAS

150 small silver sequins   Sewing needle
2 stitch holders   and thread

GAUGE

22 sts and 30 rows = 4 in. (10 cm) in St st on US 6 (4.00 mm) needles

TO FIT

Women's size Medium

SKILL LEVEL

Advanced

FINISHED SIZE: 4 in. (10 cm) wide, 9 in. (23 cm) long

RIGHT GLOVE

Rows 1–16: Using US 3 (3.25 mm) needles and A, CO 48 sts and work 16 rows of K1, P1 ribbing.

Rows 17–22: Change to size 6 (4.00 mm) needles and work 6 rows of St st with A.

Row 23 (RS): K9 with A; K5 with C; K34 with A (this places position of chart).

Rows 24–26: Work in St st from chart.

Row 27: K4 with A; work chart over 15 sts; with A, K5, inc in next st, K1, inc in next st, K21. (50 sts)

Rows 28–30: Work in St st and cont chart over 15 sts.

Row 31: In colors as set, K24, inc in next st, K3, inc in next st, K21. (52 sts)

Rows 32–43: Work in St st, cont chart, and on every 4th row K1f&b at each side of thumb for gusset as set. (58 sts)

Rows 44–46: Work in St st with A.

THUMB

Row 47 (RS): K38, turn and leave rem sts on st holder, CO 2 sts.

Row 48: P16, turn and leave rem sts on st holder, CO 2 sts.

Rows 49–55 (RS): Work in St st for 7 rows. BO kw.

With RH needle, pick up and knit 2 sts on each side at base of thumb, knit across sts on first st holder.

Next row: Purl across sts, then purl across sts on second st holder. (48 sts) Starting with a knit row, work in St st for 8 rows.

FIRST FINGER

Next row (RS): K31, turn and leave rem sts on st holder, CO 1 st.

Next row: P15, turn and leave rem sts on st holder, CO 1 st. (16 sts) Starting with a knit row, work in St st for 7 rows. BO kw.

SECOND FINGER

With RH needle, pick up and knit 2 sts at base of first finger, K6 from first st holder, turn, and CO 1 st.

Next row: Purl across these 9 sts, then P6 from second st holder, turn, and CO 1 st. (16 sts) Starting with a knit row, work in St st for 7 rows. BO kw.

THIRD FINGER

Work as for second finger.

LITTLE FINGER

With RH needle, pick up and knit 2 sts at base of third finger, K5 from first st holder.

Next row: Purl across these 7 sts, then P5 from second st holder. (12 sts)

Starting with a knit row, work in St st for 7 rows. BO kw.

LEFT GLOVE

Rows 1–22: Work as for right glove.

Row 23: K34 with A; K5 with C; K9 with A (this places position of chart).

Rows 24–26: Work in St st from chart.

Row 27: With A, K21, inc in next st, K1, inc in next st, K5; work chart over 15 sts; K4 with A. (50 sts)

Rows 28–30: Work in St st and cont chart over 15 sts.

Row 31: With A, K21; inc in next st, K3, inc in next st, K24. (52 sts)

Rows 32–43: Work in St st, cont chart, and on every 4th row K1f&b at each side of thumb for gusset as set. (58 sts)

Rows 44–46: Work in St st with A.

THUMB

Row 47 (RS): K34, turn and leave sts unworked on st holder, CO 2 sts. Finish thumb and fingers as for right glove.

BELL FRILLING ON CUFF (OPTIONAL)

Using US 3 (3.25 mm) needles and A, with RS facing, pick up and knit 40 sts evenly along CO edge of rib.

Purl 1 row.

Row 1 (RS): K1, *P3, K1; rep from * to last 3 sts, P3.

Row 2: *K3, P1, rep from * to last 4 sts, K3, P1.

Row 3: K1, *P3, YO, K1, YO; rep from * to last 3 sts, P3. (58 sts)

Row 4: *K3, P3; rep from * to last 4 sts, K3, P1.

Row 5: K1, *P3, YO, K3, YO; rep from * to last 3 sts, P3. (76 sts)

Row 6: *K3, P5; rep from * to last 4 sts, K3, P1.

Row 7: K1, *P3, YO, K5, YO; rep from * to last 3 sts, P3. (94 sts)

Row 8: *K3, P7; rep from * to last 4 sts, K3, P1.

Row 9: K1, *P3, YO, K7, YO; rep from * to last 3 sts, P3. (112 sts)

Row 10: *K3, P9; rep from * to last 4 sts, K3, P1.

Row 11: K1, *P3, YO, K9, YO; rep from * to last 3 sts, P3. (130 sts)

Row 12: *K3, P11; rep from * to last 4 sts, K3, P1.

BO all knit sts kw and all purl sts pw.

FINISHING

Weave in all ends and carefully press. Join edges of thumb and fingers and edge of glove tog. Decorate ends of fingers and thumb with silver sequins.

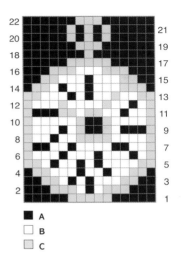

■ A
□ B
▨ C

CHOICE IS YOURS

The glove could be knitted without the motif and then be decorated with sequins or beads for an entirely new look.

DESIGNED BY CAROL MELDRUM

Firecracker Mitts

Cozy mittens worked in a colorful intarsia pattern will keep your hands warm and stylish.

YARN

Rowan *Scottish Tweed 4 ply* (100% wool; 25 g; 110 m)

A: 1 ball of color 13 Claret

B: 1 ball of color 10 Brilliant Pink

Rowan *Kidsilk Haze* (70% kid mohair, 30% silk; 25 g; 210 m)

C: 1 ball of color 596 Marmalade

D: 1 ball of color 600 Blueberry

NEEDLES

US 6 (4.00 mm) knitting needles

US 3 (3.25 mm) knitting needles

GAUGE

---

22 sts and 30 rows = 4 in. (10 cm) in St st on US 6 (4.00 mm) needles with 1 strand each of Kid Silk Haze and Scottish Tweed held tog

---

TO FIT	**SKILL LEVEL**
Women's size Medium	Intermediate/Advanced

FINISHED SIZE: 4 in. (10 cm) wide, 10 in. (25 cm) long

GLOVES (MAKE 2)

Using US 3 (3.25 mm) needles and 1 strand each of A and C held tog, CO 49 sts.

Row 1: K1, *P1, K1; rep from * to end. Change to 1 strand each of B and D held tog.

Row 2: P1, *K1, P1; rep from * to end.

Row 3: K1, *P1, K1; rep from * to end.

Rows 4–18: Rep rows 2–3 another 8 times.

Change to size 6 (4.00 mm) needles.

Row 19: Knit to last st, K1f&b. (50 sts)

Row 20: Purl.

Row 21: K2, *YO, K2tog, K2; rep from * to last 2 sts, K2.

Row 22: Purl.

Rows 23–26: Work from chart for 4 rows.

THUMB

Inc for thumb, keeping patt correct.

Row 27: Work 23 sts in patt, K1f&b, work 2, K1f&b, work patt to end. (52 sts)

Row 28: Work 25 sts in patt, P2 using B and D only, work patt to end.

Use separate bobbins of yarn A and C held tog for right and left sides. Thumb sts are knit in yarns B and D held tog throughout.

Row 29: Work 25 sts in patt, K1f&b, K4, K1f&b, work in patt to end. (54 sts)

Keeping patt correct, inc for thumb gusset as set in previous rows until you have 62 total sts.

Next row (row 16 of graph): Work 25 sts in patt, work 12 sts of thumb gusset, turn.

Work on 12 sts only.

Next row: Purl.

Work 10 rows in St st or until required length, ending in a purl row.

Next row: K1, *K2tog; rep from * to last st, K1. (7 sts)

Break off yarn, leaving approx 6–8 in. (15–20 cm); thread through sts and draw tog. Secure yarn and sew sides tog. Rejoin yarn, pick up 2 sts at base of thumb, and complete row 16 of chart.

Next row: Keeping in patt, work 24 sts, P2tog twice, work to end. (50 sts)

Complete chart.

Work 6 rows in St st using yarns A and C only.

TOP SHAPING

Next row: K1, skpo, K20, K2tog, skpo, K20, K2tog, K1. (46 sts)

Work 3 rows in St st.

Next row: K1, skpo, K18, K2tog, skpo, K18, K2tog, K1. (42 sts)

Work 3 rows in St st.

Next row: K1, skpo, K16, K2tog, skpo, K16, K2tog, K1. (38 sts)

Next row: Purl.

Next row: K1, skpo, K14, K2tog, skpo, K14, K2tog, K1. (34 sts)

Next row: Purl.

Next row: K1, skpo, K12, K2tog, skpo, K12, K2tog, K1. (30 sts)

Break off yarn.

FINISHING

Weave in all loose ends. Block and press. Sew up side seams, taking care to match up pattern. Make twisted cord and thread through eyelets.

Try exchanging the twisted cord for a silk ribbon or similar material to add a touch of elegance to the design.

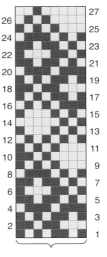

□ A and C
■ B and D

Cabled Muff

This muff is designed to be worn with cuffs outside, but for extra warmth, tuck them inside for a double thickness. The built-in storage pocket is handy for small items.

YARN

2 balls of Rowan *Cashsoft Aran* (57% merino wool, 33% microfiber, 10% cashmere, 50 g; 87 m), color 01 Oatmeal

NEEDLES

Set of 4 US 7 (4.50 mm) double-pointed needles or 2 US 7 (4.50 mm) circular needles
Set of 4 US 6 (4.00 mm) double-pointed needles or 2 US 6 (4.00 mm) circular needles

EXTRAS

Cable needle
Size F (3.75 mm) crochet hook
Decorative button
Stitch marker

GAUGE

16 sts and 28 rows = 4 in. (10 cm) in St st on US 7 (4.50 mm) needles

TO FIT

Women's size Medium

SKILL LEVEL

Intermediate

FINISHED SIZE: 5 in. (12.5 cm) wide, 16 in. (40 cm) long

PURL STITCH

1

2

3

4

1 Hold the needle with the stitches in your left hand, with the loose yarn at the front of the work. Insert the right-hand needle from right to left into the front of the first stitch on the left-hand needle.

2 Wrap the yarn from right to left, up and over the point of the right-hand needle.

3 Draw the yarn through the stitch, thus forming a new stitch on the right-hand needle.

4 Slip the original stitch off the left-hand needle, keeping the new stitch on the right-hand needle.

5 To purl a row, repeat steps 1 to 4 until all the stitches have been transferred from the left-hand needle to the right-hand needle. Turn the work, transferring the needle with the stitches to your left hand to work the next row

- -

INCREASING AND DECREASING

Many projects will require some shaping, either to add interest or to allow them to fit comfortably. Shaping is achieved by increasing or decreasing the number of stitches you are working.

INCREASING

The simplest method of increasing one stitch is to work into the front and back of the same stitch.
On a knit row, knit into the front of the stitch to be increased into; then before slipping it off the needle, place the right-hand needle behind the left-hand one and knit again into the back of it (inc). Slip the original stitch off the left-hand needle. On a purl row, purl into the front of the stitch to be increased into; then before slipping it off the needle, purl again into the back of it. Slip the original stitch off the left-hand needle.

DECREASING

The simplest method of decreasing one stitch is to work two stitches together.

On a knit row, insert the right-hand needle from left to right through *two* stitches instead of one; then knit them together as one stitch. This is called knit two together (K2tog).

On a purl row, insert the right-hand needle from right to left through *two* stitches instead of one; then purl them together as one stitch. This is called purl two together (P2tog).

INTARSIA STITCHES

Intarsia is the name given to color knitting where the pattern is worked in large blocks of color at a time, requiring a separate ball of yarn for each area of color.

DIAGONAL COLOR CHANGE WITH A SLANT TO THE LEFT

DIAGONAL COLOR CHANGE WITH A SLANT TO THE RIGHT

VERTICAL COLOR CHANGE

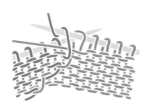

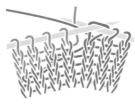

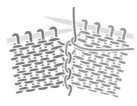

On a wrong-side row, with the yarns at the front of the work, take the first color over the second color, drop it, and then pick up the second color underneath the first color, thus crossing the two colors together.

On a right-side row, with the yarns at the back of the work, take the first color over the second color, drop it, and then pick up the second color underneath the first color, thus crossing the two colors.

Work in the first color to the color change; then drop the first color and pick up the second color underneath the first color, crossing the two colors over before working the next stitch in the second color. Work the first stitch after a color change firmly to avoid a gap forming between colors.

DOUBLE CROCHET (DC)

1 Start by wrapping the yarn over the hook and insert the hook into the fourth chain from the hook, yarn over, draw 1 loop through the work.

2 Yarn over, draw through the first 2 loops on the hook, yarn over, draw through the remaining 2 loops on the hook; 1 loop on the hook. This is 1 double crochet.

3 When you reach the end of the row, make 3 chains. These count as the first stitch of the next row. Turn the work and skip the first double crochet of the previous row; insert the hook into the second stitch of the new row. Continue to work until the end of the row, inserting the last double crochet into the top of the turning chain of the row below.

1

2

BASIC TECHNIQUES

As well as working from right to left in rows, crochet can also be worked in a circular fashion (referred to as working in the round), or even in a continuous spiral to make seamless items such as hats, bags, and other rounded objects.

MAKING FABRIC—WORKING IN ROWS

1

Make as many chain stitches as you require. This row is called the base chain. Insert the hook into the second chain from the hook (not counting the chain on the hook) for single crochet or the third chain from the hook for double crochet (fig. 1).

2
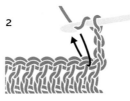

Work from right to left, inserting the hook under 2 of the 3 threads in each chain.

When you reach the end of the row, work one or more turning chains, depending on the height of the stitch.

3
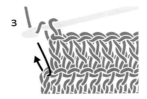

Turning chains should be worked as follows:
Single crochet: 1 chain
Half double: 2 chains
Double: 3 chains
Treble: 4 chains

Now turn the work to begin working on the next row (remember to always turn your work in the same direction). When working in single crochet, insert the hook into the first stitch in the new row and work each stitch to the end of the row, excluding the turning chain. For all other stitches, unless the pattern states otherwise, the turning chain counts as the first stitch; skip 1 stitch (fig. 2), and work each stitch to the end of the row, including the top of the turning chain (fig. 3).

MAKING FABRIC—WORKING IN THE ROUND

1   2

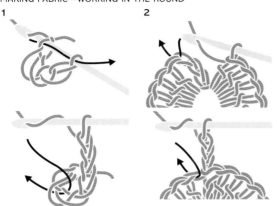

1 Crochet in the round starts with a ring. To make a ring, make a series of chains and join the last chain to the first with a slip stitch.

2 To make the first round, work a starting chain to the height of the stitch you are working in. Then work as many stitches as you need into the center of the ring and finish the round with a slip stitch into the first stitch.

3 Begin the second and subsequent rounds with a starting chain (worked the same way as a turning chain, with the number of chains depending on the stitch you are working; see page 92). Then insert the hook under the top 2 loops of each stitch in the previous round. At the end of the round, join to the top of the starting chain with a slip stitch as in step 2.

INCREASING

As with knitting, fabric is often shaped by increasing the number of stitches in a row or round. To increase, simply work an additional stitch into the next stitch. A single increase is made by working 2 stitches into the same stitch. You can increase by more than 1 stitch at a time.

DECREASING

SC2TOG
To decrease 1 stitch in single crochet (sc2tog), insert the hook into the next stitch, yarn over, draw through the work, insert the hook into the next stitch, yarn over, draw through the work, yarn over, and draw through all 3 loops, leaving just 1 loop on the hook.

SC3TOG
To decrease by 2 stitches in single crochet, work 3 stitches together (sc3tog) by working as for sc2tog until you have 3 loops on the hook, insert the hook into the next stitch, yarn over, draw through the work, yarn over, and draw through all 4 loops.

DC2TOG
To decrease 1 stitch in double crochet (dc2tog), yarn over, insert hook into next stitch, yarn over, draw through work, yarn over, draw through 2 loops, yarn over, insert hook into next stitch, yarn over, draw through work, yarn over, draw through 2 loops, yarn over, and draw through all 3 loops.

FINISHING

Fasten off your work and sew the seams together.

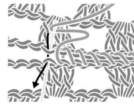

FASTENING OFF

Cut the yarn, leaving roughly 5 in. (13 cm). Make 1 chain, draw the tail through the chain, and pull firmly. Weave the end an inch in one direction, and then back the other way for a neat and secure finish.

OVERCAST STITCH

This seam creates an almost invisible join. Lay the 2 sections right side up with the stitches aligned. Insert a tapestry needle under the lower half of the edge stitch on one section, and then under the upper half of the edge stitch on the opposite section.

Abbreviations and Glossary

KNITTING ABBREVIATIONS

approx = approximately

beg = beginning

BO = bind off

CC = contrasting color

cn = cable needle

CO = cast on

cont = continue

dec = decrease

dpn = double-pointed needles

inc = increase/increasing

K = knit

K2f&b = knit into front and back of same stitch

K2tog = knit 2 stitches together

kw = knitwise

LH = left hand

M1 = Make 1 stitch. Lift the horizontal strand between the stitch just worked and next stitch, then knit through back of this thread.

MC = main color

P = purl

P2tog = purl 2 stitches together

patt = pattern

pm = place marker

prev = previous

psso = pass slipped stitch over

pw = purlwise

rem = remaining

rep = repeat

rev = reverse

RH = right hand

rnd = round

RS = right side

sl = slip

sm = slip marker

skpo = slip 1 stitch knitwise, knit 1 stitch, pass slipped stitch over

sppo = slip 1 stitch purlwise, purl 1 stitch, pass slipped stitch over

ssk = slip 1 stitch knitwise, slip 1 stitch knitwise, knit 2 stitches together

St st = stockinette stitch

st(s) = stitch(es)

tog = together

TS = thumb section

tbl = through back of loops

WS = wrong side

YO = yarn over

CROCHET ABBREVIATIONS

ch = chain

dc = double crochet

hdc = half double crochet

sc = single crochet

sl st = slip stitch

tch = turning chain

KITCHENER STITCH

With the stitches on two parallel, double-pointed needles, make sure that the working yarn is coming from the back needle. Take the tapestry needle through the first stitch on the front needle as if to purl and leave the stitch on the needle. Next, go through the first stitch on the back needle as if to knit—leave this stitch on the needle. Keeping the working yarn below the needles, work 2 sts on the front needle, followed by 2 sts on the back needle across the row as follows: On front needle, go through the first st as if to knit and drop it off the needle. Go through the second st as if to knit and leave it on the needle. Tighten the yarn. On the back needle, go through the first st as if to purl and drop it off the needle. Go through second st as if to knit and leave it on the needle. Tighten the yarn. When there is only one stitch on one needle, go through the front stitch as if to drop it off the needle. Go through the back stitch as if to purl and drop it off the needle. Pull the tail to the inside and weave in.

Resources

Debbie Bliss Yarns
www.knittingfever.com

Jamieson & Smith Ltd
www.jamiesonsshetland.co.uk

Lana Grossa
www.lanagrossa.com

Noro Yarns
www.knittingfever.com

Rowan Yarns
www.knitrowan.com

Twilleys
www.twilleys.co.uk

Indianapolis
Marion County
Public Library

Renew by Phone
269-5222

Renew on the Web
www.imcpl.org

For General Library Information
please call 269-1700

WITHDRAWN

11/10/14